METIVIER ON

Saratoga, Glens Falls, Lake George, & the Adirondacks

ૐ

Don A. Metivier

SAGAMORE PUBLISHING
Champaign, Illinois

Production supervision and interior design: Susan M. Williams
Cover and photo insert design: Michelle R. Dressen
Proofreaders: Phyllis L. Bannon and Brian J. Moore

Photo Credits: Sagamore Hotel; Walter Grishkot; Dan Way; Don A. Metivier; Chapman Museum; Office of the Mayor, Glens Falls, NY; George S. Bolster Collection; Monty E. Calvert; New York Racing Association; Saratoga Performing Arts Center; Dianne L.T. Metivier; R. Kerry Metivier; Bruce Cole.

Library of Congress Catalog Card Number:92-82550
ISBN: 0-915611-60-0

Printed in the United States.

This book is gratefully dedicated to Anthony Henry Metivier, who I thought was a wondrous father, only to learn he was just practicing to make being a grandfather an art form, and his Irish bride, Grace Ann Callahan Usher, who in addition to being a caring mother, took time to develop and support the ideas of a son who wanted to write. Without their union of 51 years, none of this would have been possible.

———————————— ❧ ————————————

CONTENTS

&

ACKNOWLEDGMENTS

This book could not have been written without the assistance, support, and encouragement of a great number of people, some of whom provided active support with ideas, information, facts, aided in research, and found and loaned pictures. A great number of others helped tremendously by living interesting lives and creating many of these stories.

To try to thank them individually would be impossible. However, a sense of fairness and the manners my folks and the good nuns taught me, and the thought I might want to do something like this again, drives me to try to mention some. If your contribution has been overlooked, it is not that it is not appreciated, but has fallen victim to a mind that gets older each day and fails to remember anything that did not happen at least a decade ago. I can vividly remember the Mohican Market, but not what I was sent to the store for this morning. That said, let me mention some of those who assisted in the research, writing, and editing of this effort.

In my career I have been blessed to work for giants as publishers. Arthur P. Irving was publisher of *The Glens Falls Times* when it hired an ambitious young reporter and provided him encouragement, support, and a living for his family while he ran around the world finding stories. He was followed by Carl R. Davidson, publisher of *The Post-Star* in my semi-mature years as a writer and columnist. He continued to support my travels, writing, and lack of attention to the day-to-day job of putting out a newspaper. I would like to gratefully acknowledge the contribution of the *Post-Star* for permission to use some of the material previously published in my column. Of late I have been given more encouragement than I am due by the publisher of this book, Joe Bannon, an old East Ender who went on to better things. His determination I would finish this task, on schedule, was the impossible dream, but he made it come true.

This book is filled with Saratoga stories, and for many of those I need to thank Shirley Day Smith, who has been a friend and supporter from her station in the New York Racing Association press office for many years. Many trainers, riders, stable hands, owners and other writers helped me learn about the wondrous world of the Saratoga backstretch, especially a trainer named Lucien Laurin, a groom named Eddie Sweat, a horse named Secretariat, and an Indian named Harry Downey.

I learned about the ballet from Shaun O'Brien, soaked up music from Bill Rice, had a lot of encouragement and help from an old pal, Ed Lewi, and the two guys who ran the show at Saratoga Performing Arts Center, Craig Hankinson and Herb Chesbrough—who someday will convince me there was a good piece of music written in the 20th century.

No single group helped me over the years and provided more stories than my friends, the cops. I have known and ridden many miles with some great ones: Bill Preston and his partner Gus Fiore; Ed Pratt; Don Walker; Alex Macura; Henry McCabe; Joe Lewis; Bill Kiernan and all the "Brains" from the old Moreau BCI; Hank LaLonde; Bob Lilly; Carl Carlton; Ted Kusnierz; Ralph W. Emerson; Hap Hayes; Don Whalen; Stan Wood, who has been involved in many of my best escapades; and my favorite Irish cop, Big Jim Duggan. Thanks as well to the many judges, attorneys and court clerks who helped me fill many notebooks with interesting material.

Thanks to Ted Kauffman, who taught me that all witches don't fly on brooms, Bob Flacke, Sr. who saved the Lake Placid Olympics and kept a hometown writer informed, and the Marzola brothers, Nick and Tom, who made sure a lot of information made its way to my typewriter.

I have worked with many talented photographers, and some of them helped with this book, especially Walter Grishkot, who searched his wondrous files for things we needed, and my old partner in the hard news business, the best newspaper shooter in the world, Monty Edward Calvert.

We had the help and assistance of many other people, including the staff at the Chapman Museum; Bruce Cole and others at the area's finest informational resource, Crandall Library; Pam Warren at the Sagamore; Glens Falls Mayor Frank O'Keefe; and trumpet players Dick Casselli and Bob LaFara.

Thanks also to the skipper of the old boat Calliope, John Hendley; and our crew who gave me enough trips on Lake George to be content and time ashore to get this task done.

My Group, which continues to grow with the arrival of husbands, wives, significant others, and grandchildren, one of whom made his entrance during the writing of this book, and my bride, Laraine, the woman who cares for all of us, were their usual supportive and innovative selves, reminding me on a daily basis of the schedule we were supposedly following and keeping me to it. A special word of thanks to my business partner and oldest son, R. Kerry, who not only worked his computer magic on the text, took pictures, and held the production schedule on track, but kept our business, Media Matters, operating, and groceries on the table while I hid away playing Hemingway.

To all mentioned and the hundreds not, we extend our heartfelt thanks for your help in making a good idea reality.

D.A.M.
August 1992

INTRODUCTION

This book is a collection of stories about interesting people, places, and events in the Saratoga/Glens Falls/Lake George/Adirondack area that the writer has been fortunate enough to know or learn about from those who did know and live them.

I have a world-class view from where I sat to write most of these stories. I can watch the old boat Calliope bob at its mooring, the waters of Harris Bay stretch across to Cleverdale, and the Adirondack Mountains rise up from the shores of the magnificent lake the English named for their king, changing it from the name St. Isaac Jogues had given it for his King. I hope some of the joy I have from this has seeped into the text.

The special places where these stories take place, Lake George, Saratoga, Hometown U.S.A. and the mountains that surround us make up a wonderful part of the world. Each of the adjacent areas has its own cast of characters, its own personality, and thankfully, its own stories.

While this is a very historical area, this is certainly not an historical book. The stories it contains are mostly separate unto themselves and have no relationship with each other except that they all occurred in this interesting part of the world.

You will find I enjoy the backstretch in the morning more than the races at Saratoga, the character of the performers more than the shows at Saratoga Performing Arts Center, the countermen at the Palace Lunch over dinner parties at Canfield Casino, the companionship an old dog can give, family, and special times with good people. I hope you will, too.

D.A.M.

1

SARATOGA IS SPECIAL AT NIGHT

≥⋒

The tourists enjoy Saratoga in the afternoon, when the ponies dash for cash, and your social status is judged by the location of your Turf Terrace table in relation to the finish line.

The insiders enjoy Saratoga in the morning. Dawn workouts of the frisky thoroughbreds, owners with sports cars parked on stable lawns, breakfast in the horseman's kitchen, it's heady stuff.

But at night they all come together. The groom in his Ford pickup, the tourist in the Saab and the owner with his BMW convertible, they all converge to enjoy the unique pleasures of Saratoga at night.

There are the parties with a guest list a hostess in Monaco would envy. Great tents filled with catered food from Michael's and music by a Duchin band. Tents on the lawns of the Racing Museum, in the back yard of the Reading Room, in the rose gardens at Yaddo.

There are socialites in designer gowns who show up in a Bentley with dates in hand-tailored tuxedos to eat chicken with their fingers at Hatties.

Saratoga at night is a long line out the door at Ben and Jerry's where the Vermont ice cream has taken hold in a city that used to live on strawberries and cream.

Saratoga at night is stopping by the spring in back of the bottling plant to partake of the radium-filled water that bubbles from the earth and watching to see if anyone glows in the dark.

Saratoga at night is hoping to get one of the few tables at Siro's not occupied by a rich young man with loafers and no socks always accompanied by a bevy of beautiful companions, and the satisfaction of sitting at one of the tiny tables quaffing a bit of the bubbly watching those who envy your seat drink their beer.

Saratoga at night is getting a seat at the yearling sales, of seeing the slightest movement of an Irish trainer as he bids up a son of Secretariat, and finally taking a breath as the numbers on the tote board above the sales ring top a million dollars. There is a unique rush caused only by standing in front of a sales stall, a Fasig Tipton catalogue under your arm, sipping champagne and listening to an owner tell his agent why the family stable needs the tiny filly eating sugar from his hand. When he says, "Buy her," it is a command General Patton would have admired.

You may have had breakfast in one of the horseman's kitchens in the backstretch, lunch on the Reading Room porch and dinner at the patron's club in the Hall of Springs before walking down to your seat in the amphitheatre for a Philadelphia Orchestra concert, but a champagne nightcap at the bar in the Gideon with some of the "boys in the band" from Philadelphia, can still make your day. As exciting as it is, nothing will ever approach that same scene when Maestro Ormandy was still a part of it. When he would raise his glass, say goodnight to the tiny group and leave for his suite upstairs in the great old hotel, all knew that a legend, a national treasure had been in their midst.

Saratoga at night is getting the first delivery of the Racing Form at the newsroom on Lake Avenue, driving along Broadway at 2 a.m. with the top down, finding a new beer to drink and discuss at the Parting Glass.

There is something very special about driving into the backstretch after midnight with an owner, drinking cheap beer from a can as an old groom talks about how a colt is responding to some "Saratoga Care" while an old dog sleeps peacefully in a nearby stall with a million-dollar runner.

Horse racing is one of the last outposts of real sportsmen. People who are in the game because they love the feeling they get when a horse they bred charges down the longest stretch in racing to win at Saratoga, or at least gave it a great try.

Saratoga at night is walking with the crowds on Caroline Street. Here is the melting pot of America. Young people in shorts and tank tops, others their same age in classic L.L. Bean khaki shorts and golf shirts from the Desert Princess Country Club. Middle-aged men in linen slacks and sea island cotton button-downs, their women in classic summer print dresses admired by the tourists in their leisure suits and chemically-based fibre slacks.

Saratoga at night is getting a rare burger on the patio at the Firehouse, a great sun dried tomato pizza at Bruno's, watching the kids groove to the sounds downstairs at the Metro and going upstairs to hear some mellow jazz with contemporaries.

Saratoga at night is dancing to a society orchestra in the cavernous Hall of Springs or the nostalgia-filled Canfield Casino, sipping coffee with some much-too-rich cake at the Rip, midnight supper at Spector's or a game of darts for a pint of Harp with some Irish trainer in the back room of "the Glass."

Saratoga at night is talking backswing at the Saratoga Golf Club, sipping a Pimm's and talking ponies with the polo crowd, or arguing the merits of Magen's Bay on St. Thomas vs. St. Tropez with anyone sporting a deep tan.

Saratoga at night is sitting at a beat up picnic table in the side yard of the old brick home owned by the Brownell sisters, a Victorian holdout against the creeping commercialism of Colonel Chicken. Sipping jug wine with Irish mime Shaun O'Brien; one of the nation's best people photographers, Chris Alexander; a couple of old cats; and assorted characters who drop by for a time; and watching a night-blooming cereus have its eight hours of spectacular life, then fade away at dawn for another year.

Horses are the main theme at Saratoga in the summer, music is the underbeat. The horses are on Union Avenue, music is everywhere. The Philadelphians are the focal point, but there is music all over town. Jazz, blues, and a bit of swing for the old timers, rock and roll for the young set, dance music for the parties, and old timers like Ida Hill for the real Saratoga crowd. Ida has been playing music for more than 60 summers in Saratoga; early on at the great clubs like Piping Rock, Brown's, and the beach clubs, and in later years at inside spots like the Union Coach House and Rick's.

Saratoga at night, sounds, places, people that all combine to make it a special place. But, like the cereus, it only blooms once a year.

☙

2

THE SAGAMORES

و

Sagamore is a good, old Indian word that has been used to describe a street in the East End of Glens Falls, the publishing firm foolish enough to bring you this book, and the last of the lavish resort hotels that used to dot the shoreline of Lake George.

When the lavish, restored Sagamore on Green Island at Bolton Landing re-opened in June, 1985, it carried on a tradition that began on July 1, 1883, when the first Sagamore Hotel opened at that storied location.

The first Sagamore was one of the world's most beautiful resort hotels. It was built by a group of Philadelphia businessmen who formed the Green Island Improvement Company. Robert Glendenning, William Bement, E. Burgess Warren, and George Burnham purchased the island for the princely sum of $30,000. That was thought to be a tremendous amount to pay for an island in Lake George, because a few years earlier, the same island had been sold for $600.

The Philadelphians were joined by John Simpson of New York, and he soon became president of the new development group.

The original Sagamore took full advantage of the setting afforded by the surrounding Adirondack Mountains, Lake George and its islands. There were exciting and differing views from the hotel, because it was built on several levels. The inside halls were spacious and open to allow the sun to stream in for much of the day. The guest rooms were on the upper levels, and many had private balconies where visitors could marvel at the lake that Europeans likened to Italy's Como.

Expansive lawns stretched out from the main buildings, and flowers lined the walkways. The first Sagamore was truly an elegant summer home for the social and wealthy of the East, many of whom were brought north from their previous summer haunt, Saratoga.

Only the rich and famous could afford the Sagamore's rates of $25 a week, a sum that was more than a month's pay to most of the working class.

The Newport and Saratoga crowd had always referred to their lavish summer homes built at the resorts as "cottages." The term came to Green Island as the four original investors built their cottages for summer living. Bellevue, Nirvana, Wapanak and East Cottage became a part of the grounds on Green Island, and the guest list for the hotel and the private cottages soon rivaled those at both Newport and Saratoga.

On June 27, 1893, a fire started in the laundry of the great hotel. It burned slowly, but before it could be contained, it roared out of control, and the massive, 10-year-old hotel was destroyed.

Myron O. Brown, who had left his position at the Mohican House to operate the Sagamore for the investors, rallied his forces, and work started at once to build the second Sagamore.

The new hotel rose three to four stories above the lake. There were more balconies, and a tower became part of the Bolton skyline. Many large trees were planted on the island, more flowers were put in place, and when the new hotel opened a year after the fire, it was not only one of the most beautiful in the nation, but many thought one of the most modern of any of the great resort hotels.

Guests were amazed to find electric lights, an elevator, private baths, and even a bowling alley.

Critics of the day were soon writing that the hotel built on the tiny island in Lake George was one of the great resort hotels of the world.

All was well with the Sagamore for another 20 years. Guests filled its rooms, enjoyed afternoon tea, evening parties, dances, and the guest list was right out of the social register of New York and Philadelphia.

Then, on Easter Sunday, 1914, fire again reduced the great hotel to ashes. The official cause was listed as careless smoking. Whispers around Bolton were that someone had torched the Sagamore.

The owners moved quickly so as not to miss the 1914 summer season. They upgraded the large building built just the year before to house the employees. Despite efforts to make the employee housing as comfortable as possible, it was far from what the guests were used to, and it was evident a new hotel would have to be built, and quickly.

A major problem, the need for a golf course, was solved with the purchase of land on Federal Hill and the construction of a quite challenging course.

It took an enterprising young man, Ernest Van Rensselaer Stiles, and a bold business deal to get what was termed a "clubhouse" built on the site. Stiles offered the owners a deal where he would take over the ruins, get a new building in place, be open by June 22, 1922, and be given stock for his efforts. By mid-June the work was done. The new "Clubhouse" had 100 rooms, 50 baths, and large public rooms. It was furnished by M.L.C. Wilmarth, owner of the famed Glens Falls furniture store, "Wilmarth's." He was a man who was to play a tremendous role in the future of the Sagamore.

The owners made do with the enlarged clubhouse for several seasons, but a new major stockholder, Dr. William Becker, wanted to rebuild the Sagamore into a luxury hotel. He brought Karl Abbott of Florida in to manage the clubhouse, and Abbott made a good profit from a newly-formed catering service. They began work on the new 200-room hotel on October 1, 1920, which proved to be a terrible time to start such a project.

On October 29, the stock market crashed, and with it, apparently, the hopes of finishing the hotel. Abbott would not quit. He got long-time Lake George summer resident William Bixby of St. Louis to buy out Dr. Becker and to put up funds to finance the construction.

By spring, the third Sagamore was finished, another 100 rooms that would return the hotel to its glory days.

The rooms were built, but they were empty. There was no money to furnish the new hotel. Enter Glens Falls furniture store owner M.L.C. Wilmarth. He furnished the bare rooms with great taste, bringing in excellent furniture. Wilmarth also provided liberal terms that the owners could afford.

On July 1, 1930, the third Sagamore opened, fully furnished, and was soon a haven to the wealthy summer visitors and to the boating crowd of Bolton residents who lived in their cottages along the lake.

The hotel was open to the public, but was more of a clubhouse for the great and gracious wealthy summer residents of the Bolton area for many years.

Following World War II, it remained open for many years, but never regained its popularity with the rich and famous. Working-class Americans were discovering a new resort style—motels—and the great resort hotel fell on hard times.

Then in the mid 1980s, the Sagamore was restored to its early elegance. It rose again, not from the ashes of a fire, but from the ashes of neglect. The fourth Sagamore has taken its place amidst the mountains and the lake with its islands as one of the world's truly fine resort hotels.

ॐ

3

THE TOWN DOG

Today he would be a public menace. He would be prosecuted by the rules of OSHA, the regulations of the New York State Health Department, and the leash law of the City of Glens Falls. He would be picked up by the animal control officer and sent to his reward in bone heaven.

But, in the late 1940s and early 50s, Timmy was the official, unofficial city dog. "He was a short-haired mixed-breed," his former personal physician, Dr. George Wiswall remembers. Doc Wiswall should know, he took care of Timmy for years and made his dog's life one of the best in town.

No one remembers where Tim came from. He just sort of appeared one day in Bank Square, took charge of his "turf," made some important friends to take care of his most urgent needs, and settled in as a permanent resident of Downtown Glens Falls.

During the late spring, summer, and early fall, he slept on the sidewalk, close to the buildings at the corner of Ridge and Warren Streets. He was especially fond of the sidewalk in front of the Warren Pharmacy, where he could catch the afternoon sun.

When he was hungry, the cop who was on his beat in Bank Square would see him standing near the curb in Warren Street. The officer would know to stop traffic and get Timmy across the busy street to the Palace Lunch, where Tim regularly took his meals. The door to the Palace did not open in or out, but it slid to the side. When a patron slid the door open to enter or leave, Tim would quickly scamper through; in all his years, that sliding door never closed on his beefy flanks.

Timmy knew the schedule at the Palace. He never showed up during the busy times. Early mornings, when half the town was there for breakfast, Tim was still catching up on his rest in a doorway. During the crazed noon hour when all of downtown had to eat in 60 minutes, Tim was elsewhere. He may have taken a bus ride, been asleep in the back of a cruising police car, or found a ray of sun on a sidewalk and worked on his tan.

Timmy wandered over to the Palace about mid-morning for his breakfast, carefully looking over whatever Earl, or Tucker, or Mert put down for him. He loved Saturdays, which were chicken pie days at the Palace. Thursday was not for him. The customers loved shells and meatballs every Thursday, but Tim was not into Italian food.

Today there would be a major problem with Timmy eating at the end of the lunch counter. Someone would file a class action suit claiming their child was harmed by having to eat in close proximity of a dog with terrible table manners, bad breath, and gas. But in those days, Timmy would gobble up his meal and check out the space between the row of stools and the counter with its thick glass top to see if any careless diner had dropped anything interesting.

His post-meal nap in the corner at the end of the row of stools, his loud snoring, and other sounds would violate a lot of rules and regulations about animals in restaurants and public places. However, to the Palace lunch crowd, which was made up of working stiffs, cops, most of city government, a priest or two from St. Mary's, and any kid lucky enough to have been taken there for a meal or a piece of the world's best pie, Timmy was just one of the regulars. Another with the good sense to show up at the Palace at mealtime.

When Timmy got bored with the comings and goings of Bank Square, or downtown got too crowded—don't laugh, Downtown Glens Falls used to get full—he would board one of the Hudson Transportation Company buses and take a ride. He usually got on the Glen Street bus and rode for one trip, getting off on the opposite side of Warren Street, never going to Hudson Falls. Timmy was known to ride the Depot bus from time to time, taking a tour of the East End, would ride on the Belt Line, and every once in a while would go up the South Street line. "He never rode the Broad Acres bus," Driver Bernie Tracy told us once, "he wasn't a Broad Acres kind of dog. He was more at home on the Belt Line."

There were times when Timmy would eat too much, or get too much sun, and pharmacist Len LaBarge, who operated the Warren Pharmacy, would note that the pup was a bit under the weather. Len would take Timmy out to the Glen Street bus and tell the driver to leave him at Dr. Wiswall's at the end of the run near Woodbury's. As soon as Doc Wiswall had worked his magic and was sure old Tim was in top shape again, he would bring him out to the bus stop, and the next driver by would take him back to Bank Square.

In addition to taking "rides," Tim would go on a vacation once or twice a year. "You always knew when Tim was bored and wanted to get away," Patrolman Jack LaFara would tell visitors. "He would howl a little, get one of us cops to cross him over Warren Street, and instead of going into the Palace, he would get on the bus to Fort Edward. I don't know how he knew the difference between the Hudson Falls bus and the Fort Edward bus, but he always went to Fort Edward on vacation."

When Tim got to Fort Edward he would get off the bus at the railroad station, hang around, get a few meals, sleep on the platform and just hang out and see a lot of new people for two or three days.

Once Timmy had had enough of vacation and Fort Edward, he would sit on the curb at the corner and get on the next bus bound for Glens Falls.

In the winter, Timmy would sleep inside at the Warren Pharmacy, or along the wall behind the last couple of stools in the Palace. Tim loved the warm weather; he tolerated the cold, but as Hap the Counterman told a group of customers in the Palace one cold January day, "If old Tim knew you could get a bus to Florida, we would never see him here in the winter."

While Timmy had a lot of nodding acquaintances, he had only a few close friends: Len LaBarge, the Palace lunch crew, a few of the older cops, like Jack LaFara or Happy Hayes, and the Bank Square regulars such as Hymie the Tailor, David the Shoeman, bar owner Ben Hoey, Doc Cook, and the other bookies who operated their horserooms across Warren Street from each other.

Old Tim was one of the few who knew what the wire was, stretched across Warren Street, from one window above Schulte's

Cigar Store to another above David's Shoes. It was "the wire" that connected both horserooms with the outside world of race tracks and baseball stadiums.

One day, a truck filled with new Dodge cars went down Warren Street, headed to the Ford Garage—of course the Ford Garage sold Dodge cars, but that's a whole other story— and the top car on the trailer pulled the wire down. Patrons poured out of the second floor horserooms into the street; all of Tim's closest friends were howling, and so was he. The cop in Bank Square had to climb up onto the car on the trailer and put the ends of the wire back together. As soon as the results were flowing again, the Square quickly emptied, and Tim got back to chasing the sun in front of the Pharmacy.

Timmy was a true local character. He was a part of Downtown Glens Falls. He slept on its sidewalks, walked the beats with its cops, rode its buses, patronized its veterinary hospital, and took his meals in its favorite diner.

There is a stone container on a Manhattan sidewalk in front of a jewelry store. It says "Dog Bar," and it is filled with cool water for any dog being walked along the avenue. Glens Falls should construct a similar "Dog Bar" in Bank Square and dedicate it to "Timmy, Hometown U.S.A.'s Own Dog."

ટ

4

COPS AND ROBBERS

Among the most happy times of a happy career were those years when I wrote cops and robbers. Being a police reporter in a small town during the time when cops and reporters were friends and not adversaries, was educational, fun, and sometimes exciting.

We can lump educational and fun into one story. I was riding with an officer one evening when we noticed a young priest walking up South Street, suitcase in hand, obviously a newcomer who had just arrived at the Trailways bus station on his way to a new job at St. Alphonsus up the street. As we waited for the light, we saw him reading the signs in the window of the then-toughest bar on the street.

"He thinks he can eat there," the cop said, as he backed the patrol car down the street and pulled to the curb. "Father, hey Father," he called as the priest was opening the door to a place where the cops went in pairs, if at all, and the visiting lumberjacks settled disagreements with chairs and beer bottles.

We took the newcomer to a diner, bought him supper, and a few months later he was officially the chaplain of the Glens Falls Police Department. It was a task he took quite seriously, always making himself available for counseling or just some needed conversation with cops and their families.

He always told the story of being "saved" from trying to get supper at a gin mill where most of the food served came from glass jars filled with old eggs. His other favorite story was about the night he was riding with the same patrolman who had welcomed him to town and they answered a disturbance call to a Maple Street watering hole. When they walked in they found two matrons settling an argument.

It seems both claimed their mammary glands were the largest in the place. To settle the dispute, they had brought out a scale and were weighing their more than ample breasts on the bar. "I thought I had seen it all," the priest would laugh in re-telling the story, "but you have to realize there is always something new at the end of every call you answer."

For excitement, there was the night I was riding with an officer who shall remain nameless, and we answered a call for a "big fight" at a Maple Street bar. When we arrived, there were a couple of guys rolling around on the sidewalk, each trying to do bodily damage to the other.

Separated, we got them into the back seat of the police car just as a patron ran out of the bar and shouted, "Some guys are beating up someone in the alley."

Handing me his gun, the cop said, "You keep these perps here, I'll check out the alley." He disappeared into the darkness, nightstick in hand, as I told the two cowering in the police car I was more afraid of him than I was of them, "so don't even think of leaving."

Just about then the same customer who had brought news of the alley fight reappeared and told me, "If you don't want your friend to get killed, you had better get into that alley and help him."

After quickly explaining to the two combatants in the car it would be in their very best interest if they were there when I returned, I hurried into the alley. My friend the cop needed no help but the three guys laid out on the bricks did. So much for my rescue.

The cop who handed me the gun knew I couldn't hurt anyone with it while he was gone. He had seen me in action on the range. Each summer, members of area police agencies spend a week on the range, honing their skills with an assortment of firearms. Everyone must qualify with whatever weapon they carry, which at that time was a regular .38 calibre revolver for the street cops, and a snub-nose for the detectives. I never qualified with anything, and every summer would win the funny trophy offered for "The Worst Shot." I have a collection.

There were times when I wished I had paid more attention to Captain Ralph Waldo Emerson, the range officer. One such was an evening riding with Detective Bill Preston, one half of the Preston/Fiore Team that made "Good-Guy, Bad-Guy" policing an art form. Photographer Monty Calvert had gotten interested in firearms, loaded his own bullets, and could hit what he pointed at, why couldn't I, and where was Monty when I needed him?

Preston and I were riding along Glen Street in "one-eight," which was a huge ark of a car the department must have gotten on sale and gave to the detectives. Every perp in three counties knew that car, they might just as well driven a vehicle with a sign on the side, "Glens Falls Detectives," because that thing was one of a kind, and they were stuck with it. The only redeeming feature it had was that the back window went down, and Preston could carry lumber in it when he needed a quick delivery at some carpenter job he was doing in his off time.

As we neared the First National Bank—Glen Street still had two-way traffic then—we noticed some guy reaching into the night depository. We pulled over and watched for a minute, and this guy was obviously trying to take something out of the depository, and the rules are that this is where you put things into the bank, no withdrawals.

There had been a problem with someone opening the depository, stuffing something into the chute, waiting for a customer to toss a money bag into the night drop, and then going into the depository, grabbing the cash, and making a hasty exit to some warm bar to spend it.

The cops had watched the bank from time to time, but never did catch the thief pulling his routine. Preston and I were sure we were watching him. The detective radioed for some uniformed guys to visit our location on Glen Street, but the guy at the bank chute looked over, apparently recognized the car, and slammed the depository door shut.

Preston stepped out of the car into Glen Street, and the guy on the sidewalk directed his attention to him. It was then that I realized Preston had a gun, and I had a pencil and a notebook. If the perp on the sidewalk shot Preston, I had better make a friend, or try to remember the Act of Contrition the nuns taught me. For some stupid reason, I opened the door, and yelled at the guy. If I can distract him, I thought, Preston wins, ergo, I win.

"Hi," the local businessman we both recognize says, "that damn depository didn't drop my bank bag inside. I was trying to push it down." I breathed again, and that damn Preston laughed; my scenario had gone through his mind too. We took the guy for coffee, but we never told him we were trying to surround him with two guys and one gun.

Another of my other "thrills" in police work occurred one evening as I was driving out Corinth Road to pick up a few of my young skiers at West Mountain. I noticed a Queensbury Police car at the side of the road and saw a familiar face wrestling with three guys. Just like in the movies, I stopped. For some stupid reason I took a ski pole that was on the back seat and went down the road to help. I rapped one guy alongside the head with the ski pole and got him onto the ground, while the cop took care of the other two. We had all three combatants on the ground, when out of the darkness came this older man leading a group of about four younger guys. Each carried what looked like a club or a hunk of wood.

Sitting on my bad guy I looked at the still-struggling cop, and I remember saying: "George, we are about to get our clocks cleaned."

The old man spoke the most reassuring words I have ever heard: "What's happening here George, you guys need a hand with these freaks?" The cop and I smiled at each other like the settlers must have smiled when the Cavalry arrived to chase the indians away.

Soon scads of other police units were there, the three fighting drunks were taken away, and peace and tranquility returned to Corinth Road. The cop and I offered our thanks to the old guy and his hulking sons as they returned to their nearby home.

I certainly had a story to tell the kids on the way home. They were not impressed.

ॐ

5

DOC COOK

ða

"Where are your old comic books?" the oldest boy who is now also my business partner asked. "Didn't you have a lot of Superman, Donald Duck, and Classic Comics?"

Knowing he must have read the story I had seen in the newspaper that morning about the value of old comic books, and knowing we had bought the first round of computers that run our office with funds secured by the sale of my baseball cards, I realized he was not asking because he wanted to read about Donald Duck or Clark Kent.

"Yes, I had lots of Superman, Donald Duck, and Classic Comics 1 to 141, but your Grandfather gave them to Doc Cook when I was away at college," I told him.

"Doc Cook, Doc Cook," he raged, "who the hell was Doc Cook?" I realized I had neglected his education.

Elwyn C. Cook was a famous character in a town filled with great characters. Glens Falls had "Bronco" Charlie Miller, the last of the Pony Express riders, Hymie the Tailor, the Blind Indian and Doc Peck, a magician friend of Houdini, but in all of these Doc Cook stood well in front.

He came to Glens Falls because of the illness of his wife. They rented a home at Kattskill Bay, not far from the home of the famous Hanneford circus families. Mrs. Cook's condition became worse, and she entered Westmount Sanitarium for treatment.

Doc Cook had come to Glens Falls from New York City, where he had been in show business. He served as a foil for the famed comedian Joe Cook and traveled the vaudeville circuit for many years.

He later moved to the Lake Sunnyside area, and residents remember him walking the several miles to Glens Falls every day, his derby hat in place, his smartly pressed suit sporting a fresh carnation in the lapel.

Few knew how famous he really was, but his scrapbook reveals Doc Cook was a tremendous theatrical personality. Standing in a floor-length white fur coat, clutching his famous umbrella and wearing a bowler in a picture on the front page of the scrapbook is the man Doc worked with for many years, the great comedian Joe Cook. The pair were appearing in the Earol Carroll Vanities in New York. Doc noted alongside the picture: "October 12, 1923, the day what's his name discovered America, and the Giants beat the Yanks 1-0, as Casey Stengel hit his second homer."

Inside the front page is a picture of the famous dancer Sally Rand wearing only two of her famed fans and a big smile.

An inscription shows Doc knew the top people in vaudeville: "Doc will always remain as a fond memory of our bright days in vaudeville long after we are gone," wrote Gus Edwards on December 19, 1923. Ever the clown, George Jessel wrote: "To my old friend Doc Cook, from his young friend, Georgie Jessel."

Heywood Broun, one of the earliest Broadway columnists who made drinking a synonym for newspapermen wrote: "To Doc Cook, for medicinal purposes only."

"Merry Christmas to Doc Cook," wrote Jack Dempsey, and an autographed picture of President Calvin Coolidge marks the time Doc played the White House on February 29, 1924.

One of the finest tributes to Doc came from the star of the Palace show in April 1924, as Irma Claire wrote: "My sincere good wishes to the laugh Doctor, whose medicine never fails." Eddie Cantor penned: "To Doc Cook, stay out of jail."

Doc Cook gave up being a vaudeville star to bring his wife to Glens Falls for her final days. Despite the fine treatment she received at Westmount, she passed away, but her husband never forgot the kindness shown his beloved wife at the facility.

During his daily visits to Westmount to visit her, he saw that the patients did not have much entertainment, so he developed a program of taking entertainers to the facility and later made the shows a memorial to his wife.

Jimmy Cotter of Glens Falls worked with Doc along with many volunteers. Cotter, one of the most knowledgeable circus writers in the world, took care of the publicity for the Cook shows, and served as master of ceremonies from time to time.

Local entertainers along with the professionals playing at such spots as Tony Reed's Royal Pines, dancers from every studio in the area, the nationally known magician Dr. Gordon Peck of Glens Falls and of course all the members of the Hanneford family, including world famous Poodles and Gracie, were regulars at Westmount.

Dr. Lyman Thayer, director at Westmount, used to tell his colleagues in the medical profession that Westmount was an unofficial stop on the vaudeville circuit.

Doc Cook continued promoting shows at Westmount for years, making sure there were special performances at every holiday.

He had help from everyone. Cars were always available to bring the performers to the facility, and if the cast was large, Hudson Transportation Company would give Doc a bus. One day Cotter missed his ride and made a phone call. He was told to wait in front of Ben Hoey's Shamrock Grill on Warren Street. "A few minutes later a big black limo pulled up, and this tough guy driver leaned out the window and told me to get in. I knew better than to ask who owned that car," Cotter remembers.

You see, Doc Cook wrote numbers for a living. Before the State of New York ran the horse rooms and wrote the numbers as a lottery, the numbers were the poor man's bet. Doc took numbers bets all over Glens Falls, working for the local front men of the Piping Rock Club in Saratoga.

He made a good living, and spent it all on the kids at Westmount. In later years, Doc Cook rode on the back of the Glens Falls Police Department's three-wheel motorcycle, collecting nickels from the parking meters. It also helped his old legs get around town to collect his own nickels on the numbers. It was a good arrangement, the city had an honest employee who turned in all the parking money, and Doc had a ride around town to collect from his customers.

One of his great treats in life was Halloween. Doc would go from bar to bar, trick or treating every bartender. He would start out at Ben Hoey's, see Louis at the Globe Hotel, Clarence Daggett at the Commodore, Ed O'Niel at the Queensbury, hit the Wonder Bar and the Madden, and then Joe Lawler and Ken Usher at the Esquire before winding up with "Bum" Kelleher on Elm Street. The Doctor would be flying as high as any Halloween witch when the police car finally came to take him home.

Doc Cook had a signature song, which he sang at his shows. He used to sing it to me in the back room of my grandfather's meat market as he sat at the card table arranging his betting slips for transportation to Saratoga. I don't remember it all, but I know it closed: "I am the celebrated Doc Cook. The toast of Paris, a hit in Rome, a smash in New York, but a flop here at home."

He was anything but a "flop" with the kids at Westmount, which is why I can't get too upset with my father for giving him those now thousand-dollar comic books.

&

6

10-4 IS CODE FOUR

❧

It was a sunny Sunday afternoon and the group was in the massive backyard where I had grown up, enjoying the above-ground swim facility their grandfather had scrounged and saved to buy for them.

This collection of sheets of aluminum with a plastic liner was the focal point of the playground he and my mother kept for them. When "Grandpa Mitch" knew that any of the group was planning on using the pool, which he regularly filled with the garden hose, he would lug pails of warm water from the house and dump it in the pool, "...to take the chill off."

He would then sit in one of his favorite chairs amidst the swing sets, basketball backboard, and pitching mound left over from my days as a backyard athlete, puff on his cigar, and enjoy the noise that only kids having fun can bring to an old man's yard.

One of the twins was making an above-water appearance for air when a parakeet landed on his head. "That's funny," he remarked, "it feels like there is a bird on my head."

The oldest boy, the family one-line champion, hit him with a classic. "That's because there is a bird on your head."

We have no idea where this brightly colored bird came from. He was not seen flying around, he just zoomed out of a tree near the pool onto the first head that appeared above the water.

The poor bird tried to fly away, but was quickly captured by several still dripping swimmers, who caged him in a shoebox. Not being able to find a bird cage in Grandpa Mitch's shed, a building that they believed in their hearts had one of everything in the world somewhere in its mess, they dressed and began scouring the neighborhood for a real cage.

Success! A classmate had recently suffered through the passing of a canary and would like nothing better than to get rid of the cage, its toys, and cover, which brought only bad memories of better days.

The parakeet came home, was placed in its newly borrowed cage and was officially dubbed the family pet. "Until we get a dog," the oldest boy mumbled.

Now when you get a new pet a lot of the fun is giving it a meaningful name. Not something dumb like "Tweety" or "Cleo," but a name that fits its ownership group and home situation.

A holdover from my days as a police reporter was a police radio scanner that still held forth on all eight channels, 24 hours a day from its permanent home on the kitchen counter. We had the only kids on the street who on hearing a siren ran inside to hear where the fire or other happening was taking place and who was being sent to take care of it.

After so many years you don't even hear the barrage of talk from the eight busy channels unless it really says something important. The babble of radio repair checks and coffee orders for the station becomes part of the background noise regularly created in a house filled with seven kids and now a bird.

We noted the radio was near the bird's cage and the transmissions were not old hat to him, but voices without explanation. So, the thought was developed to name the bird "10-4," "...then everytime somebody says 10-4 on the police radio he'll think they're talking to him."

He loved it. When the kids were all in school, the radio would jabber away and the bird chirped back at the hundreds of "10-4s" that soon became part of his background noise.

News of the monitor-listening bird spread and in the quiet hours of the morning you would hear the police-like voice of a bored deputy or ranger or city cop coo, "10-4s a good bird, 10-4s a good bird," and from under the cover of the cage would come a chirp back to the unknown friend on the radio.

Just how accustomed he became to lots of noise and the babble of the radio was not apparent, until we went away for a week of skiing and left him at the grandparent's house. "He just sat there in the cage," grandmother reported to the calling children at midweek, "until I realized he needed some noise. I put a radio near him and we left it on, he picked right up. If he gets bored again, I'll call Chief Duggan and have him ride around in a police car for a couple of hours to catch up on his radio friends." There is no wondering where the kids got their sense of humor.

There was the day he got loose when the neat twin was cleaning the cage. He walked across someone's peanut butter sandwich and then landed on the baby's head. Have you ever seen a baby with peanut butter footprints on her head? Funny does not cover that situation.

Then he landed on the living room drapes and walked along them over the picture window. Mom's drapes with peanut butter footprints on them also does not get covered by "funny," but for other reasons.

After several years of chirping at the police radio and leaving his mark around the house, 10-4, the happy bird, got terribly quiet. He sat for hours in the corner of his cage, didn't look into his mirror and didn't even kick around the little plastic bird that he totally dominated for nearly two years.

The cardiologist who regularly attends our New Year's Eve party looked at him and said that while he didn't see too many parakeets, 10-4 did not appear to be the picture of health. We took him to the vet, and the mother of the house gave him the prescribed medicine twice a day. Despite the efforts, on a Sunday afternoon, 10-4 went Code 4.

Returning from an apple-picking expedition to the Town of Hampton, the family found him lifeless in his cage. With appropriate ceremony, he was buried, his plastic friend with him, in the cardboard box that was selected from the girl's closet. He was buried in the family pet burial ground with "George" a turtle, various goldfish, and a squirrel that had fallen from the telephone wire into the driveway two years ago.

I never knew 10-4 had served in the military, perhaps it was because of his unofficial membership in several police agencies, but I noticed this week a small American flag had joined the pet rock headstone that marks his backyard grave. Questioning the flag's owner about decorating a bird's grave with such a symbol we were asked the ultimate question: "How would you like to be buried in a box that said Dexter's?"

&

7

GOOD MORNIN'

ॐ

"Backstretch Kitchen Open," the hand-lettered sign nailed to the old elm noted. Saratoga, one of the oldest and certainly the most beautiful race track in North America was coming alive for another racing and social season.

There were only a few horses on the main track. It had rained overnight, and their hoofs slapped against the mud with a smacking sound that carried across the backstretch in the early morning stillness.

The assistant trainers gathered along the backstretch rail, carefully watching the workouts, paying as much attention to the works of the thoroughbreds from other stables as they did their own.

All offered the universal Saratoga greeting: "Good mornin'." The exercise riders did the same as they passed on mounts that pranced excitedly as they walked across the stable lawns toward the muddy oval, or gulped in huge breaths of the humid air with their flanks covered with mud and sweat heaved from the effort of a recent workout. The ones going out looked forward to doing what they had been bred to accomplish, run as fast as the little person on their backs asked them to go. The ones coming in, filled with the rush of accomplishment, look forward to the coolness of the barns, the cleansing soak of a bath, and a hot walk under the century-old trees to cool down.

Saratoga wakes up slowly after its winter and spring of inactivity. It gathers momentum for the short season when it becomes the center of the thoroughbred racing universe, and then just as quickly closes down to await another August, another season.

But now it is wake up time, and the excitement is just beginning to build. Tractors pull carts loaded with brush for the jumps in the infield steeplechase course. Flowers grown during the winter in the greenhouses near the Oklahoma training track are planted. Ivy reaches down the front of the clubhouse from boxes at sites that have held flowers and ivy to please Saratoga patrons for more than a century.

Grass that is green and lush is everywhere, in the saddling area of the paddock, in the picnic areas, through the parking lots, and certainly in the infield. There are those who point out the parking and the walkways would be more efficient if the grass was gone, and practical paving was put in its place. If old trees that take up valuable space were removed, there would be more badly-needed parking spots. All this is dismissed as just so much thoughtless heresy by real Saratoga followers. This special place was not designed by engineers, but by sportsmen. It is not supposed to be coldly efficient; there are too many places like that already, but there is only one Saratoga.

The old clockers click their stopwatches to catch the times of the early morning workouts, and talk about the Saratoga of long-ago, seeing the ghostly shapes of Whirlaway, Native Dancer, Buckpasser, Secretariat, Affirmed, and the others winning races like the Jim Dandy, the Sanford, the Whitney and the famed mid-summer derby, the Travers.

Trucks loaded with hay trundle into the grounds, dropping bales at the empty barns that will soon be filled with nervous thoroughbreds. The stalls are clean, a pile of fresh straw covers the floor. A new flypaper hangs from the rafters, the ground outside has been raked and picked of pebbles that could harm the tiny feet that carry race horses down the long Saratoga stretch.

Fifty-gallon drums sit on concrete blocks, old red pumps primed alongside. Soon steam will rise from the water as it heats in the barrels, as a warm, sudsy bath awaits each sweating runner returning from a morning run or an afternoon race. Sure, there is a new hot water system that is supposed to replace the cumbersome barrels, but somehow the old stables still light a fire or two and do it the old way, so the charm remains. They heat the water with a propane burner fed from a tank tied to a nearby tree, and that is a grudging concession to modern horse training, since many of the old hands would still use a wood fire if it were allowed.

The sounds of portable radios blare from tackroom doorways, their reggae music another intrusion into the post-bellum atmosphere of the Saratoga backstretch. The barns stand where they were first built, as John Morrissey's idea for a track along Union Avenue was a post-Civil War development. The older ones still sport moss-covered slate roofs, the newer ones asbestos shingles. A remodeled building sports a garish aluminum cover that glints even in the grey of the overcast dawn.

As you walk under the trees past the empty stalls awaiting the big horse vans that will soon begin pulling in from off the nearby Adirondack Northway, the smell of Absorbine, horse liniment, suddenly fills the air. Around the corner a teenage girl gently rubs the hot, tired legs of a filly fresh in from her morning cantor. "Hi" she answers to your greeting. An old groom mucking a stall turns to her and says, "Up here girl we always say good mornin'." Her Saratoga training has begun.

You can hear the excited jabbering of the cooks and the dishwashers in the horseman's kitchen even before the old screen door bangs closed behind you. "Good mornin', good mornin'," they shout as you walk up to the food line. "So good to be back up in Saratoga, how was your winter? It's nice to see you," the old kitchen boss says putting out a bony, black, friendly hand. "Ella, this man likes his eggs over, lots of potatoes. You give Mr. Don his coffee, boy," he tells his grinning grandson. There is only one place on earth like this.

The smells of the baked ham, frying eggs, browning toast, and fresh brewing coffee mingle into an aromatic delight. Talk on the porch over plates of eggs and home fried potatoes, stacks of pancakes, and endless thick mugs filled with strong coffee centers on family, baseball, how green the grass in the infield is this season, how well the New York football Giants will do, and of course, horses.

The cook comes out to chalk up the first day's menu on the old blackboard near the door. "Meal - Baked ham or roast pork - $3.25." She backs off and reads it aloud. More to herself than to those sitting on the porch at the old wooden picnic tables with their faded oilcloth covers, she says: "We had to do it. Sorry honey, we had to raise that price." Last year "the meal" was $3.

Looking out at the assembled group, a few exercise riders, grooms, assistant trainers, a writer and his photographer, and a couple of owners, all wolfing down breakfast, she explains it all. "Inflation, that's what done it, in...flation."

Saratoga is waking up, the horses are coming, and soon every afternoon, 25,000 or more people will fill the stands across the way. They don't know about the real world of Saratoga back here among the trees with the pumps and the barns and the kitchen with its great smells.

Time to go back to watch the works. As we leave, the teenage girl who had been rubbing the colt comes in. "Good mornin'" she nods. You smile. You feel good. This place, this Saratoga will survive.

ᨓ

8

THE HALFWAY HOUSE

a.

The few that remember the Halfway House on Route 9 talk about its great food and marvelous hospitality. Some even remember the obscene parrot who used words now favored by comedians, but then not usually used in public.

The Halfway House, legend has it, was located halfway between Glens Falls and Lake George, as well as halfway between Montreal and New York City. Records show the first eating place at the site, opposite where Route 149 leaves Route 9 for its journey east into Washington County, was a tavern that was in existence in 1825.

An early settler named Udney Buck ran the tavern that was actually located across the road from where the Halfway House was to stand. There was a gate and a toll road that continued to Lake George, and the Tally Ho coaches used to stop for fresh horses, and the passengers on their way to Lake George would grab a meal and an ale or two.

A later owner of the tavern, George Brown, took over in 1846 and started building the original part of the Halfway House on the opposite side of the highway.

Brown was a famous host at the restaurant; his hospitality kept the customers coming, and the name of the restaurant made it one of the most popular in the Adirondacks. Brown ran the place until at least 1884. It continued under several owners, and in 1915 was purchased by Arthur Lyle. He made the restaurant famous for his hospitality and for Mrs. Lyle's cooking, and the phrase that marked the place, "known from coast to coast," was coined.

Perhaps the best known of the owners, Daniel J. Hurley, took over from the Lyle family and operated the Halfway House until December 1, 1943, when he was forced to close because of travel and food restrictions caused by World War II.

While most remember visiting for the food, which featured chicken and wondrous steaks, I have a recollection of being taken there by my grandfather, who labored in the kitchens as the chief butcher. I learned about rare New York strip sirloins and crispy chicken skin long before such items became the bane of those seeking a healthy diet.

While memories of the dining room, the magnificent porch and the music of the orchestras are hazy, I remember being taken to see my father at work across the road in the "annex" like it was yesterday.

He ran a table, and it wasn't covered with food. Its surface was covered with numbers, and a big wheel spun at one end where a little ball dropped in a slot to select a number. My grandfather's rich French accent made the term "roulette" sound like music.

My dad was quite a sport in his shiny black shoes, spats, white linen pants, and a nicely tailored sport coat. A gold watch chain looped across between the pockets of his vest. Today he would be called a pit boss, but in those kinder, gentler times he was a table director.

The main room of the Halfway House "annex" was home to the roulette and craps tables; there were slot machines along the walls, and in a separate room some friendly, if high stakes, card games.

The annex and the casino at another Route 9 restaurant, Fan and Bill's, were operated by some tough guys out of Saratoga. The two spots were only open in the summer tourist season, although the slots got distributed around town for the winter. There were always a couple of machines in the back room of my grandfather's meat market. I remember they used to keep an old milk crate, made from heavy wood with steel holders for the milk bottles inside, next to the slot machines. The nice old lady who sold insurance door to door would come by a few times a week to try to make a profit on the nickels she had been collecting on her debit route. She was so small she had to stand on the milk crate to reach the slot. Obviously, she was the reason they kept the milk crate there, because I was not allowed to put the nickels the guys in the card game used to give me from the pots into the slots.

The Halfway House opened following World War II and quickly became a popular eating house. More than 200 persons were enjoying dinner at 1:15 a.m., on Sunday, May 5, 1946, when a small fire was started by sparks from the kitchen exhaust fan. It caused little alarm. Waiters continued to carry the roast chicken and the strip sirloins out into the dining room for the late night suppers.

Manager Roger Gottleib, two chefs, and other employees tried to extinguish the fire as it raced into the roof over the kitchen. Dining room captain Erskine E. Chaffin used a hand extinguisher on another area of the kitchen, but the fire was winning.

Bernie Collins and his Orchestra, playing the first night of a spring engagement, picked up their instruments, pushed the piano to the great porch and left. Soon, patrons were asked to leave. Many wanted to take their meals with them. There are those who swear the parrot yelled to the hostess, "Hey you ..., don't forget me," but others say it's just a good story, and that the bird was not there after the war.

An hour later, the 100-year old Halfway House "known from coast to coast" was destroyed. Firemen from Lake George and Glens Falls, assisted by pumpers from South Glens Falls and Warrensburg, fought a losing battle, as the landmark burned down.

Flames shot 75 feet into the air. Persons at Lake George said the flames reflected off the water of the lake. Spectators drove up from Saratoga, where, they said, an orange glow could be seen in the sky during the height of the inferno.

Crowds stood on Route 9 at the foot of French Mountain, at the site that today houses a Dexter Shoe outlet, and watched the landmark disappear. A Glens Falls fireman narrowly escaped death as the roof collapsed, and he rode the timbers down into the flames below, where his colleagues pulled him out.

There was talk of rebuilding the restaurant for a time, but nothing ever came of it. During March, 1948, the New York State Department of Public Works purchased slightly more than one-tenth of an acre of the Halfway House land to widen Route 9. On March 19, 1948, the state announced that the construction on Route 9 would be done by the Department of Public Works and not private contractors. "There has been no date set for the start of work," a spokesman said.

There still hasn't. Probably the feasibility study hasn't been completed.

&

9

A FAIRY TALE

ን

Once upon a time there was a little girl living with her mother in Miami, and like most little girls she had the normal dream of growing up to be a famous ballerina, meeting a handsome prince and living happily ever after.

For Colleen Neary that fairy tale deam came true, the prince came along, and the happy ever after started following the New York City Ballet season in Saratoga in 1979.

Colleen was the youngest of the two Neary girls. Their father died when they were young, and their mother had to work very hard to bring them up and help them realize their dream of becoming dancers. Both wanted to be ballerinas.

Patricia, the elder of the pair, was the first to realize her dream. She joined the corps of the New York City Ballet and soon became a soloist. Her younger sister worked hard to follow and when she was only eight got accepted as a student in the School of American Ballet in New York City.

Their mother moved to New York, and just as a movie script would have shown, got a job at the most New York of stores, Macy's. She maintained a home for her girls in New York as they grew in talent and stature in the demanding and over-filled field of dance.

Colleen started appearing in children's roles of ballet productions. She was seen in "Harlequinade," and "Don Quixote," when she was only 10. At 14 she discovered the magic summer world of Saratoga.

Balanchine, the ballet master and co-founder of the New York City Ballet, had made the decision to bring his troupe to Saratoga to become one of the regular summer residents of the new Saratoga Performing Arts Center for the 1966 season. Critics had scoffed at Balanchine's idea that he could teach "Upstate" audiences about the sophisticated dance form.

He persisted, saying the dancers would love the charm and relaxed atmosphere of Saratoga, and that the people of the Saratoga region would accept and support the classic company he and Lincoln Kirstein had assembled. He was right of course, and soon not only was ballet accepted and supported, but schools had popped up so all the little girls in Saratoga could follow their dream of someday dancing on the big SPAC stage Balanchine had designed.

"My sister was there for the summer season, dancing at SPAC, and she loved it, so I begged her to let me come up for the summer," Colleen Neary remembered.

Not satisfied to watch her sister and the others dance, Colleen got herself involved in a class of young dancers who practiced regularly in the historic Canfield Casino in downtown Saratoga's Congress Park.

"The mirrors in the Casino were waist high," she said, "so at the end of the summer our shoulders and heads were doing well, but our legs flopped around a lot." She persisted, and danced and trained to be a ballerina.

Soon George Balanchine didn't think the tall, strong teenager flopped around too much at all. She was only 16 when he invited her to enter the corps of the New York City Ballet and to continue her dance education in its school. Her fairy tale was moving right along.

As she matured and grew in skill and poise, her roles increased. She appeared in most of the repertory works of the company as a member of the corps and was promoted to being a soloist well ahead of schedule. Then Balanchine gave her the invitation that dancers spend a lifetime seeking. He asked her to become a principal dancer with the New York City Ballet, its loftiest slot, reserved for the best in a company that Balanchine insisted would have "no stars."

Colleen Neary danced the principal roles in such productions as the lavish "Firebird," and the first full-length Balanchine epic "Jewels."

Balanchine gave her his finest compliment when he created a role for her as the female lead in the "War and Discord" divertissement of "Coppelia," Balanchine's full-length ballet, which had its world premiere at Saratoga on July 17, 1974.

"Coppelia" was a tremendous statement by Balanchine. He choreographed the wondrous story of the doll who came to life for several reasons. To provide a vehicle for his company's longtime mime star, Shaun O'Brien, and bring to the veteran dancer/actor the fame and rewards Balanchine felt were O'Brien's due for a long and distinguished career. He also wanted several of his female principals to have a dance program that would gain attention from people other than the regular ballet audience. And he wanted to reward Saratoga for supporting ballet.

New York City critics raged at Balanchine, noting "Coppelia" was far too important a work in the genius career of the master to open at Saratoga. Balanchine, as usual, persisted. "Coppelia" was what *Variety* would label "A Smash." O'Brien was a star, and the female leads, including Colleen Neary, were discovered by large new audiences. The fairy tale was moving along very well.

As her career bloomed, Balanchine looked ahead, and encouraged her to begin teaching, because like a pro football player, a dancer's knees are not forever. She taught classes in the School of American Ballet, conducted auditions for the company around the country and was selected to teach Company classes for other New York City Ballet dancers.

The fairy tale got a boost in the summer of 1978, when she happened to pay a visit to the antique store operated north of Saratoga by the concertmaster of the New York City Ballet Orchestra, Lamar Alsop, and his wife. There was a young man in the store, a singer, who was appearing at the Gideon Putnam. Now wait a minute, you're getting ahead of me, let me finish the story.

Bobby Michaels invited Colleen Neary to come to the Gideon Putnam Hotel lounge and hear him sing. She invited him to walk down the hill to SPAC and watch her dance. They did.

He later invited her to become Mrs. Bobby Michaels. That happy event took place in the Alsop home following the ballet's summer season. As the New York City Ballet closed out its 14th season in Saratoga, Colleen Neary retired and left the company where she had spent 19 glorious years.

She and her prince charming went to Switzerland where she became the ballet mistress of the Zurich Ballet Company, under the firm hand of its director, Patricia Neary. Bobby found a new manager, bookings in Europe, and a recording career.

So the happy ever afters continue, and as Balanchine noted at the wedding, "sometimes, just sometimes, fairy tales still do come true."

ᘒ

10

THE FLOWER BLOOMS

ᶻ⋅

Dancers who a short time before had been performing to the eclectic music of Charles Ives and the carefully contrived and choreographed steps of August Bournonville, George Balanchine, and Jerome Robbins, were jumping around the main salon of the Canfield Casino to the rock and roll beat of Chuck Berry.

They had completed the grueling schedule of a July Saturday, a 2 p.m. matinee, and a completely sold out regular evening performance of the New York City Ballet on the massive stage of the Saratoga Performing Arts Center. Now it was time to play.

They had been dancing on the battleship linoleum Balanchine had chosen for the stage floor to the music of Serge Prokofiev as played by the New York City Ballet Orchestra under the skillful baton of its music director Robert Irving. Now they boogied on the marble floors of the Casino to the sounds of "After Hours," a three-piece group from Santa Fe. It featured Don Armstrong on guitar, Victoria Armstrong on piano, and a bass player from the Star-Spangled Washboard Band, Keith Stephenson.

The dancers were relaxing after two of the most successful weeks of any summer season the Company ever had at Saratoga. The young dancers from the corps, the gifted soloists, even several of the famed principals were kicking back and getting down on the fun music as guests of the New York City Ballet Guild at its annual summer post-performance cast appreciation party.

"Saratoga spritz" —white wine and ginger ale—was the drink of the evening.

Shaun O'Brien, the oldest and longest-time member of the Company, arrived and was greeted with the deference his time in grade deserved. O'Brien is one part mime actor, one part dancer, and one part leprechaun. His mother hoped he would become a priest but a sister who became a nun had to satisfy those wishes of the Brooklyn portion of the O'Brien clan.

He came to the New York City Ballet with Balanchine and has been around ever since. He has played many roles, but for seasons was best known for sitting on the clock during the Nutcracker, as VonRothbert the sorcerer in Swan Lake, and many other character and acting roles. When Balanchine recreated "Coppelia" in 1974, he wrote the meaty part of Dr. Copelius for O'Brien, and it made him a star.

O'Brien is also known for rescuing one of the swans in a Saratoga performance of "Swan Lake." As Adam Luders and Nina Fedorova danced the final scene, and a row of swans zipped across the back of the stage, one of the swans got caught and didn't leave. The audience, trying to watch the two dancers complete the wondrous story, couldn't take their eyes off the errant swan.

Gathering the capes of the sorcerer around him, O'Brien swooped down on the bird, put it under the flowing cap, and strode off the stage to the instant applause of the audience and stage crew alike.

O'Brien brought the news to the Casino. He had heard it from the Sacketts (Francis and Paul) who had heard it from Tony Blum, so you knew it was probably almost certainly fact.

"The flower is blooming," O'Brien told the tiny little group who gathered to hear the secret. "The Brownell sisters' night-blooming cereus is blooming tonight."

The Brownell sisters of Saratoga are famous among the dancers of the New York City Ballet. Retired, they live in their family home, a 19th-century brick structure surrounded on all sides by intrusions from the 20th century. "Colonel Chicken," as they call it, has a fast-food shop across the street. There is a pizza palace, a motel, and all the plastic idols of modern times, but in their midst the Brownell sisters live in general victoriana, unaffected by it all.

Among their prize possessions are two night-blooming cereus (Peruvianus) cactus plants, brought home as slips from a long-ago visit to a garden in Maine.

A night-blooming cereus has one flower a year. It develops slowly, then as darkness falls one evening, begins to bloom. By midnight, it is fully developed. It lives through the hours till dawn, then like some Transylvanian creature, falls apart, forever gone.

(An aside: My bride got a slip of a cereus, nurtured it, made it grow to a healthy plant. That was years ago. "I have never had it bloom," she told O'Brien one day as they sat in the victorian garden of his Saratoga home. "I've never seen a flower on it." "Ah," the Irish bit of nonsense smiled at her, "you've never seen it, but do you really know?" She wonders about that all the time. I have heard her asking the damn plant.)

News that this was the night, that the flower was blooming, spread throughout the Company of dancers, and many of them paid a visit to the inside garden of their vine-covered home.

The scene was not of a Saturday in modern times, but rather from a long-ago, quieter time when such things as a flower in bloom got time and attention from a gentler population.

It seemed obscene to drive to the house, but there were no carriages available. We all piled into my convertible, O'Brien sitting up on the back like a politico in a parade. We parked a block from the victorian house. O'Brien left to "check it out," to see if the show was still underway. It was well past 2 a.m., and the sisters were elderly. It did seem the thing to do, sort of knock first.

After 2 a.m. was not late for the Brownells, who were sitting in the garden with the flower. Down the street, O'Brien stood and waved his arms, a ghostly figure in his usual all-white suit. Alfred Hitchcock would have loved this scene.

We all trooped on down the road to the garden: Christopher Alexander, a witty and super talented show business photographer; Virginia Donaldson, the longtime press representative for the Company; and your servant writer and bride.

As we entered the 100-year-old garden the scene was nothing Hitchcock has ever imagined. Sitting on a battered picnic table, illuminated by candles, was the cereus. The flower was huge, as big as your head. Its white petals seemed to dance in the flicker of the candlelight.

The Brownell sisters offered wine from a jug, a hunk of cheese to slice at will, and brilliant conversation. We talked dance and music, and talent vs the lack of it, and history. The house had been built on the site by their grandparents in the 19th century.

Their parents had been married in its parlor in 1895. They had lived there, traveled, but never really left the victorian atmosphere. They resisted selling the house to developers for service stations, restaurants, apartments, and motels. They had been offered princely sums for their corner lot.

Trees, flowers, and scores of herbs filled the garden. Vines hold the house together, and keep out the too-close views of modern life that were just outside the iron fence. Only an odor of cooking chicken reached into the garden to remind us the outside world lurked but a few steps away.

We washed the cheese down with the soft wine. Christopher took a few quiet pictures, using just the candles for light. The sister muses sat with Sarah the cat and the flower.

Time stood still for a few hours, and the sisters showed us a glimpse of how things used to be in another time that Colonel Chicken will never replace.

ða

11

THE HUGHES BAN

ⓩ

On April 12, 1862, a son was born to Pastor and Mrs. David Charles Hughes of the First Baptist Church on Maple Street in Glens Falls.

Less than 20 miles away, William R. Travers and some friends were struggling to organize Saratoga Racetrack. They had no way of knowing that the baby born that day in Glens Falls would someday nearly put an end to not only their track on Union Avenue in Saratoga Springs, but the entire horse racing industry in the State of New York and in many other parts of the United States.

When the boy was two years old, Saratoga Racetrack was flourishing. It was decided to hold a major stakes race for the finest horses. The new race was named the Travers, after the first president of Saratoga Racetrack and his horse, Kentucky, took the first running of this great stakes. Kentucky covered the then-mile and three quarters in 3:18 3/4, to earn the princely sum of $2,950, much more than a year's pay for most in those times.

The Travers went on to become the unofficial fourth race of the Triple Crown, the Midsummer Derby, the real test for mature three year olds, and now, of course, the winner earns upwards of a million dollars.

It almost didn't come to pass, and all because of the boy from Glens Falls who grew up to be Governor of New York, Chief Justice of the United States Supreme Court, and the only man to win the popular vote for President of the United States and not be elected to the office.

Hughes wanted to be a jurist, and serving on the bench was his driving ambition. He was dragged into the New York State governor's race in 1906 when the Republicans gave him their nomination. He tried to decline, but reformers convinced him he was needed in Albany, not on the bench, but in the governor's mansion.

Hughes won the election, beating William Randolph Hearst by only 57,897 votes and became the Governor of New York. He was a reformer, and while the political machines hated him, his honesty and fighting spirit caught the imagination of the people who returned him to office in 1908.

His reforms rocked New York, as he created the Public Service Commission and other state agencies, taking power and patronage away from the powerful political machines that were centered in New York and Albany.

His career took him to Washington, and he missed being the President of the United States by the narrowest margin in history. He won the popular vote, but lost by 23 electoral votes to Woodrow Wilson in 1916.

Hughes was later named to the Supreme Court, and served as its Chief Justice for many years. His decisions are landmarks in the law and centered on his belief the Constitution was the law of the land. What was said was what is meant, and all law sprang from it. He also served on numerous commissions, and his contributions to the United States are boundless.

For all of this, the racing community despised him.

During his second term as Governor, it came to Hughes' attention that the New York State Constitution contained a mandate against gambling. Hughes was not personally opposed to gambling, despite his Baptist background, and his close friends noted that he did not take a puritanical attitude toward betting.

However, he felt bookmaking at horse races in New York loomed as a crass and deliberate violation of the state constitution.

Hughes believed the Constitution was intended to be the law of the land and was to be obeyed. His personal secretary, Robert H. Fuller, wrote that his feeling that the absolute rule of law came from the Constitution was the chief reason why Hughes attacked race track gambling.

Battle lines were formed. Hughes saw the struggle as a fight between right and wrong. The gamblers and the horseplayers saw it as a fight for survival.

A fight in the Legislature to stop gambling brought out the worst in everyone. Gamblers walked the hall of the Legislature in Albany, passing out $200,000 to ensure votes. Hughes' life was threatened. There were threats to kidnap his baby daughter.

Debate in the New York State Senate was terrible. Mrs. Hughes left the Chamber one afternoon in tears after hearing her husband attacked from the Senate floor.

The Legislature adjourned in open defiance of Hughes, and he called them back into special session. The Governor declared nothing less than representative government was on trial. Governor Hughes prevailed, by the smallest of margins, and he was credited with putting many New York race tracks out of business, including the famed half-mile oval back in his hometown of Glens Falls. Racing never returned to his birthplace, despite the fact that the world record for the pacing mile had been established there.

Racetracks had been popping up like dandelions all over the country. Many editorialists said the number of new tracks was nothing more than "milking" a good thing, and applauded Hughes for closing them down.

On June 11, 1908, Hughes signed the Hart-Agnew bill into law, and betting became illegal in New York. Racing staggered on for a while, betting being conducted on an oral, man-to-man basis. In 1910, the Director's Liability Act was passed, oral betting was prohibited, and on August 31, 1910, Saratoga closed. Racing was dead in New York State, thank you Charles Evans Hughes.

There was no racing in the state during 1911 and 1912, stopped by what the racing fraternity called "The Hughes Ban." In fact, in the current list of racing results for major stakes in New York, the lines opposite 1911 and 1912 note, "No racing, Hughes Ban."

Hughes was blamed for dealing a death blow to horse racing. While racing was blacked out in New York, owners and trainers moved their stables to Canada. Woodbine became famous as a thoroughbred race track.

It was written in a New York newspaper, "He (Hughes) crippled the value of the American thoroughbred when its prestige was at its height. Although racing resumed within two years, the hangover from the Hughes Ban lasted much longer."

Effects of the New York ban on gambling spread, and within 24 months, California, Texas, Louisiana, and Georgia all had anti-gambling laws.

Racing did come back in New York State and has become stronger, more popular and better run than ever. Para-mutuel betting replaced the track bookmakers and many racing insiders admit the fright of the Hughes Ban helped clean up the entire racing industry, and in the long run helped it grow to the multi-million dollar business it has become.

They remember and honor William R. Travers every third Saturday in August at Saratoga with the running of the famed stakes that bear his name. But, there is no race named to honor the person who stopped gambling and maintained representative government in New York State, the boy from Glens Falls, Charles Evans Hughes.

ᐟᐩ

12

KEEP THE FAITH

ﾞﾞ

Having outdoor parties in the Adirondacks during the summer is traditional, fun, and risky. It has been known to rain here from time to time, and the idea of a quick Adirondack thundershower dampening a group of lawn partygoers can be frightening.

It isn't just the fact that the group may get wet that bothers most of the mountain hostesses, it is the fact they may quickly move from the safety of picnic tables on the lawn to the coffee table in your living room. The thought of celebrants arriving, drinks and sloppy hotdogs in hand, inside your house, of lime cooler spilled on a tan couch, causes the hostess sleepless nights prior to the afternoon/evening of her soiree.

Plans for such a summer gathering made the weather topic number one at our place for a full week before the first guest was scheduled to arrive.

Saturday night would find a few ("this party is growing like mold on cheese, if you ask one more couple, we are moving it to the outfield at Crandall Park") friends gathering on the back lawn.

I won't say our back yard is small, but I don't mind having to mow it. And, when the kids were little, and they had a swing and a sandbox there, you didn't have to mow it.

As we worked through the week, each day of rain and the forecast of more took years off the life of a woman who had raised seven kids, a cranky dog, and a husband who writes for a living.

Trying to be supportive I pointed out: "Don't worry, Mary Lou Whitney gives these parties all the time. She never looks like she just won a honeymoon trip on the Titanic, relax."

The unreasonable reply is something about, "You rent me the Canfield Casino, hire Michael the Caterer, and give me a blank check, and I'll look like I just won the lottery all week, too."

The guest list grows. You know how it goes, she remembers someone who invited you to their daughter's after-prom parent's party, and you remember a client who needs to feel wanted. The little summer gathering is starting to get a little unreasonable in size.

Suddenly near the end of the week the atmosphere around the house changes. There is an air of calm. We get through breakfast with only some mention of how fresh the English muffins were today. Dinner brings on comments about the wine. Something is terribly wrong here.

Finally I can stand it no longer, I must bring up the subject I most do not want to talk about. "What is this with no mention of the weather. Given up hope?"

"Don't worry about it," she says, "and where did you get that St. Emilion?, it certainly goes with this beef."

Saturday dawns. It is overcast, just a little threatening, like a thin smile from an unpaid bookie. But, there is no rain.

The back yard is transformed into a miniature Fort George Park. The boys borrow a truck and move a dozen tables from West Mountain to our corner. The girls turn to and help, and someone even cleans the years of grease, soot, and old pieces of hot dog off the grill on the outdoor stove.

Afternoon arrives, the clouds thicken. Still, no mention of the weather, no panic, no problem, things just roll along like she was getting ready for our annual New Year's Eve bash where all she has to worry about is if the fondue will thicken.

The years of being a reporter finally overcome the will of a husband to never ask. "Why aren't you worried about the weather?" There, I said it.

"No problem," she smiles, "I have talked it over with the mailman. It's taken care of."

"How to calm vicious dogs, that I can understand talking over with the only representative of the federal government who visits our home every day," I tell her. "Talking to him about the weather, how to keep it from raining, unless it's a new service like Express Mail or nine-number ZIP codes, this I don't understand."

She explains. "It's simple."

"That's good," I mumble, "then I shall understand it."

"Be quiet and listen," the former nervous hostess says.

"His daughter, the mailman's daughter, was getting married. They were having an outdoor reception and it rained all week. So, on the day of the wedding, they put a rosary in a tree. Just as the reception started, the rain stopped." She looked at me with all the confidence of an apostle stepping over the side of the boat to follow Him on the water.

"You put a rosary in a tree?"

"Sure, it's over there in the ugly cedar you refuse to trim."

Sure enough, hanging next to the old nursery school birdfeeder and the kindergarten suet bag—I have to take those things down, the kid that made them is in college— was a rosary.

Alas, the night was perfect, not a hint of rain, mild. We really did have a lot of people. I thought we had plenty of tables. A lot of folks stood up. But they never had to venture into the living room.

Every time a beer spilled on the lawn, she smiled. Someone dropped their Jello salad: "Don't worry," I heard her laugh, "the old dog loves orange Jello."

A priest guest arrived. He's an old friend who knows where the good Scotch and the tough problems are kept in this house, and he's solved most of them, and done very well with the Scotch.

"A rosary in a tree! Glory be to God. I've heard it all now. I knew people who put out a statue of St. Joseph, but never a rosary in a tree."

Told it was a remedy from the mailman, he accepted it. The Deity he deals with, the feds he leaves alone.

The last cars are pulling away. She walks into the house holding the rosary mumbling something that sounded like, "I told you the mailman had the answer."

I walked outside with a couple of the boys to start picking up. It was just starting to rain. I'll never doubt a mailman again.

&

13

FLYING HIGH

ع

We all know people who won't fly. They sit home while other members of the family go winging off to ski, travel, make money, or just see the world. My father-in-law, at 88, still drives to Florida every fall and home every spring, because he doesn't trust airplanes. One daughter was with me on an airplane that should have never taken off, landed in a blizzard, and skidded sideways down a LaGuardia runway for more than a mile. If I call her and say we are going to Miami or Morocco, she will be at the airport, camera in hand, ready when they are. But her older sister, who when she was younger flew to Switzerland to ski and write, flew over the Grand Canyon in a tiny sightseeing rig, and around this country, has suddenly determined she will no longer fly. Don't invite her to board anything but the sailboat.

One of the reasons people have problems in the air is because we are completely out of the loop. The pilot flies the plane, and we follow. At least in a car we have ourselves to blame, and even if the Northway is not as safe as 35,000 feet, we feel our skills will prevail.

My first "experience" in an airplane was on a flight from Boston to Washington on the way to Charlotte to broadcast the NCAA basketball playoffs. I was still a college student and hadn't done much flying. The fact that my broadcast partner was a Korean vet named Bill Brady, who had been pretty well shot up in that "police action" gave me some comfort. We were on a DC something that had a table in the back where you could sit, talk, read, and just get away from your seat. Brady and I were sitting around the little table when the stewardess, now called a flight attendant, showed up and asked, "Can I sit with you guys?" We thought that a great idea until we saw how nervous she was. "What's wrong?" Brady asked, only to be informed that the wheels would not go down, and we were to circle the busy skis above Washington for a time. An hour later she was crying, a co-pilot had joined us for a hand-holding session, and the wheels were still up.

The flight engineer—why don't they have them anymore?—opened a panel on the floor, eventually got the wheels down and the pilot got the plane down. I figured I had experienced my thrill in the air.

Not yet! It came as we were taking off from the airport in Milan following a ski writing trip to the Italian Alps. As we gained a little altitude, the inside of the plane got dark. Since it was noon, this was a bit disconcerting, and became worse when I realized the sun was not shining through the windows because the smoke from the inboard port engine was covering the windows. The smoke gave way to flames, and the huge plane shuddered. The Alitalia pilot feathered the burning engine, and soon crew members were looking out the window at the now only slightly smoking engine. A crewman talked excitedly to the pilot on the phone. Since I was sitting at the window he was looking out of, I figured I could get some good information on our problem. I asked him, "This thing flies on three engines doesn't it?" He assured me it could fly on two if necessary. He was worried it could not fly with one wing. He thought the port wing was cracked and might suddenly drop away.

The pilot reassured us with these wonderful words: "The fire is out. We are going to attempt an emergency landing in Rome." Why did he say "attempt"?

We went down on the deck, flying so close to the water of the Med, I know people were jumping off their boats as we thundered over. The little guy with the phone never left the window. He told me later if the wing did crack, he was to tell the pilot and our flying boat would have immediately become just a boat.

Two long pipes appeared out of the ends of the wings. Suddenly liquid was gushing out of the pipes, and the guy with the phone leaned over to tell me— I guess he had to talk to someone besides the pilot— the liquid was the thousands of gallons of jet fuel that were to have taken us to New York. "We have to empty the tanks, but he has to keep enough so we can get to Rome," the phone guy said. Well, there was something for me to think about, to keep my mind off the cracked wing.

I was sitting next to an American priest, who was saying his rosary. "There are more than 250 people on this plane," I said to him. "If this thing goes down, it will be the biggest crash ever. I hope there is a radio in the life raft, I want to call my newspaper." He hit me with the rosary. Isn't that a sacrilige?

We landed 56 minutes later in Rome and got to see all the fire trucks, crash wagons, and emergency vehicles Leonardo di Vinci Airport has. When the giant 747 rolled to a stop, that's where we all got out. Standing out on the tarmac I asked an Alitalia guy in white coveralls, who climbed out of the engine after an inspection, what was wrong. He said a piece of the fan had torn loose, been sucked into the engine, and the friction started a fire. There never was a problem with the wing, there was no crack. Such good news.

They bused us into a terminal, popped some bubbly, and said there was a plane to New York in half an hour. Two hundred and forty eight people declined to go. The priest and I took the two seats they offered us in first class, and ate all the way across the Atlantic. He wore the rosary around his neck and probably still does.

For years I figured that would be my experience in the air. Wrong again.

I was standing at the gate to the apron at Warren County Airport, when I saw the speck in the sky and watched it grow into the twin engine corporate aircraft that was to take me on a business call to Hartford, Connecticut. I do not like small airplanes, but when the company says the plane will take you to Hartford tomorrow afternoon, you are there, you get on, and you go.

I knew the pilot, and when he said he had to go into the terminal to borrow a screwdriver, I did not hesitate to ask why. "There's something wrong with the catch on the door," he muttered, and after a few minutes prying at the closing mechanism, he returned the screwdriver and we were off.

We were in the air about ten minutes, had circled out over Lake George, got back on a track that I expected would bring us to Connecticut when it happened. The door at my elbow blew open. Where I had been looking at a pocket filled with maps, I was now looking at the ground far below, the maps were trailing out behind us.

I was wearing a seat belt and the little plane wasn't pressurized, so I imagined there was little chance I would be sucked out. And, I now knew that my heart was good, because when that door flew open at 250 miles an hour a mile up, it had not stopped.

The noise was amazing. I could see the pilot was yelling something to me, but I couldn't hear him above the wind and the motor noise. I finally understood he was asking for the charts. I pointed behind us and he nodded, realizing they had been blown away.

"You have to close that door, so I can land," he said over the noise. Really?, I thought. Lean out there, get hold of the door, close it, and hold it closed while we land. What a project.

Fortunately the door was flapping in the slipstream. If it had opened the other way, there would have been no closing it in the air. I got a grip on the handle and pulled. The catch was broken, but I could hold the door tight to the plane so it wouldn't flap in the wind.

I thought he was going back to the nice long runways of Warren County, but he pointed out ahead of us. All I could see was a cemetery. He leveled off, slipped toward the ground, and I made out a tiny stretch of grass. We dropped over the cemetery and onto what I thought was a lawn, only to discover Granville had an airport. It was only a grass strip, but it looked like JFK to me once I was on the ground.

"I'm going to fix the door, and we can go," he said. Good thing there was no Hertz desk at Granville International, or he would have had to hold the door himself all the way to Hartford.

⁂

14

SAMMY DAVIS, JR.

ह

A couple of us were having a late supper in a tucked-away Las Vegas restaurant, the kind of place you save for nights when you are tired and need a good meal without the glitz and noise of the Strip and its enormous dining rooms. This joint has nice French food, a strong wine list, skillful waiters, and no clanging, bell-ringing, light flashing slots.

There was a private party in the next room, a birthday party for Sammy Davis, Jr., given by his friend Jerry Lewis. A small gathering of a dozen people, enjoying each other's stories and memories of good times.

During our dinner Davis walked past, I smiled and said, "Happy birthday." He nodded a thanks, then stopped. "Hey, man," he grinned, "you're the guy who brought Tony to see me." Sticking out a thin, bony hand, he grabbed mine and brought me into his birthday party to tell stories about being a little boy in Lake George.

I was thrilled, pleased, happy but not surprised, because "Tony" had played a major role in the early life and times of Sammy Davis, Jr.

During my days of coming of age in the Lake George Region, the "in" place to be was the Rustic Inn at Lake Venare on the way to Lake Luzerne. Sure, there were joints in the Village, the Hitching Post up Route 9N and others, but the local playboys went to our classmate Don Gorman's dad's place, the Rustic Inn. There was good barroom music there. Patty Marino and Donnie Howard would play and sing and be totally outrageous, packing the place every weekend. The troopers would sit at the end of the bar, a monitor to the radio in their car at their elbow to catch calls. Everyone went to the Rustic.

Years before, the top place was the Royal Pines, located on Route 9, opposite Bloody Pond. I learned about the "Pines" from the dapper guy who held forth in the city treasurer's office when I covered City Hall. Anthony J. "Tony" Reed was far more than a good source for City Hall news and gossip, he was a direct link to the glorious past because the Royal Pines had been his.

The Pines had been a full-blown nightclub during its glory years and had attracted some of the best entertainers in the nation. One of these was there with his uncle, Will Maston, and his dad, Sammy Davis, Sr.

A yellowed clipping I have read noted the weekend program at the Royal Pines would feature the Will Maston Trio, with "Little Sunshine," Sammy Davis, Jr.

"Little Bobby Winchell" was the master of ceremonies on a bill that included singer Alice Evans and Jimmy Smith and his Kings of Rhythm band. The minimum was $1 on Saturday night, and there was no cover charge.

Tony Reed often spoke about his club on the Lake George Road, remembering the Fontaine Sisters, Cab Calloway and others, but he most enjoyed memories of a little boy, Sammy Davis, Jr. "What a talent, but he was also a great little kid," Reed used to remember. "He worked so hard, he didn't get much chance to be a little boy."

That bothered Reed, and he used to try and get Davis to take time from his singing and dancing to do the things other ten year olds did.

"He was surrounded by huge talent, but he was as good or better than any of the older entertainers," Tony Reed said, "and we had tremendous talent at the Pines. Will Maston and the Fontaine Sisters got so much attention some of the others got overlooked.

"Jimmy Smith discovered Cab Calloway, he got him into the Cotton Club in Harlem."

One night when Jimmy Rovelli was holding forth as the entertainment at the Queensbury Hotel bar, he introduced a member of the audience and brought him up to sing a couple of songs. It was "Little Bobby Winchell," and after the impromptu performance we asked him about the Pines. Winchell rattled off the names of the Kings of Rhythm like he had been singing with them last week. "Gus Parham played tenor, Clinton Walker was on piano, Arque Dickinson on trumpet, so was Bing Thompson, and Ray Cully played drums," he remembered.

For a long-time musician freak those are great names. Arque Dickinson was a regular with the great Fletcher Henderson band. That's like telling your kids someone played with the Kinks. They had to be good.

Winchell remembered THAT when Leo Reisman conducted his orchestra on the showboat on Lake George, the well-known music director would finish his shows and then hurry down the road to the Royal Pines to sit and listen to Jimmy Smith and the Kings of Rhythm. "They were his favorite band," Winchell said.

Ringside tables were always filled with notables. Boxer Bob Pastor was a regular, and in the summer all the top jockeys, trainers, and owners from Saratoga would pack the room.

The Royal Pines was in full flower from the summer of 1935 to September 1941, and then did not reopen during the summer of '42, as Tony Reed and many others were away on government jobs, fighting in World War II.

There had been a singing group there in 1936 and again in '37, known as the Ross Trio. Margie and Bea and their brother Frankie. Frankie died in a battle in Italy during 1943. After the war, the girls replaced him with another sister, Jerri, and renamed the trio the Fontaine Sisters. They got a job singing backup to a former band singer named Perry Como, and the rest, as they say, is history.

The show at the Pines changed every two weeks, except when Sammy Davis was there. He would stay five to six weeks and still keep packing them in. There were two shows a night, one at 11, the second at 2 a.m. After the summer season, most of the group moved to the Florida hotels.

One August Sunday in the late 1960s, Sammy Davis, Jr. was starring in a one-day show at Saratoga Performing Arts Center. Tony Reed was an old man, he didn't get around too good, but he was ready for a ride to Saratoga to see "Little Sunshine" perform. The old man cried as Sammy danced and sang and ran around the big SPAC stage. "He's still got more talent than anyone," Reed said to no one in particular.

Davis was doing an afternoon and an evening show at SPAC and following the afternoon performance I took Reed backstage. "Sorry," the huge bodyguard-type said, "Mr. Davis is very tired, he can't see anyone."

"Just tell him Tony Reed is here," I asked.

The hulk did not return, Davis came. He embraced the old man, hugged him for a long time, and took us to his dressing room. He shooed all the hangers-on away, and they sat holding hands, talking, remembering.

"Do you know," Davis told me, "this man bought me a football. I was ten years old and he gave me this football. It was one of the few toys I ever had. We didn't have time for things like that. He used to make the cooks go out in back of the Pines in the afternoon and toss that football around with me. He was very important when I was growing up. How I love this old guy."

They talked and once Davis got up and did a little soft shoe. "Those were my dad's steps," he smiled. Soon it was time to go, and an emotional goodbye tore up everyone backstage.

So, years later when Davis grabbed my hand in a Las Vegas restaurant, it was a rekindling of that backstage celebration in Saratoga, and a kid remembering some happy times of growing up at the Pines in Lake George.

≈

15

THE 1921 TRAVERS

ða

The annual running of the Travers Stakes, usually on the third Saturday in August, brings together the best three-year-old thoroughbreds in the world. Usually it's a bunch of colts, but sometimes an owner or trainer will have a filly they feel can run with the boys.

The Midsummer Derby, the unofficial fourth race of the Triple Crown, is filled with history, drama, and great stories. None is better than the little-known tale of the 1921 edition.

Harry Payne Whitney owned one of the great mares of all time, Prudery, and she was the overwhelming favorite to win the 1921 Travers. There was talk it might be a "walk-over," horse track parlance for a one-horse race. Most of the other owners decided they had no chance and were not planning to challenge the Whitney mare.

Arnold Rothstein, proprietor of one of Saratoga's best known gambling casinos, the Brook, also had a string of horses, as well as a silent partnership in the ownership of the Chicago Cubs. It was silent, since baseball was just getting over the 1919 White Sox scandal, and gamblers were not welcome in baseball.

Rothstein arrived in Saratoga in 1904. He was a young bookmaker and soon became enormously wealthy. Many believed he had not always played by the rules to get to the top.

Rothstein entered his horse, Sporting Blood, in the Travers, with the idea of picking up second-place money. He had learned from one of his spies working in the stable area that Prudery was acting strange and was very nervous. He quickly paid a bribe to a Whitney stable hand and discovered Prudery was not eating and had missed several workouts. A veterinarian picked up a few quid from Rothstein in exchange for the news he had examined the mare and believed she would not be at her top form for the Travers, planned for Saturday, August 20.

On the morning of the race, the odds on Prudery stood at 1 to 4, and Sporting Blood was listed at 5 to 2. There was always the possibility Whitney might withdraw the mare from the stakes.

Rothstein knew, however, Whitney was a great sportsman and unless the mare became physically ill, he would want to give her a chance to win the Travers, one of the nation's greatest horse racing tests.

Then there was an unexpected development in the race. Just before noon, Grey Lag, the year's leading three-year-old money winner, was entered by Sam Hildreth, partner of Harry Sinclair, a millionaire oilman.

The betting crowd immediately shifted its efforts to wagering on Grey Lag, and the odds on Sporting Blood grew.

Using his agents, Rothstein bet $150,000, spreading it with bookies all over the country. He got an average price of 3 to 1 on Sporting Blood.

The bookies were greedy as they saw the bets coming in on Sporting Blood as easy money, since both Grey Lag and Prudery were clearly better runners. For that reason, most of them never wired the money to Saratoga to be bet at the track, but kept the bets themselves, figuring they would make a lot of extra cash on the running of the 1921 Travers.

Less than an hour before post time, moments before the deadline for scratching, Hildreth took Gray Lag out of the race, leaving just the mare Prudery and Sporting Blood in the field.

Bettors quickly shifted their money to the Whitney mare and the odds on her dropped to 2 to 7. Since there was little on-track action on Sporting Blood, the bookies kept the money they had taken on Rothstein's horse and the odds did not change.

Prudery took the lead early and held it easily until the mile mark. Then Sporting Blood made a move. At the top of the stretch, one of the longest of any track in the nation, Prudery was in front by about half a length. As the pair came through the quarter-mile homestretch, Sporting Blood ran her down. The mare came apart and lost by more than two lengths.

Rothstein picked up $450,000 from the bookies, and the winners purse, a part of which many believed, but never proved, went to Hildreth for his part in the betting coup.

Rothstein was far from done in Saratoga sporting and gambling circles. His win in the Travers was later eclipsed by a story of his winning a stud poker hand from Nick the Greek in a Spa casino card game. The pot held $605,000 in an era when successful people earned $20 a week.

Rothstein was driven from the Spa by a reform movement and went to New York City. In 1928 he lost a card game when another player shot him dead for cheating. After his death, it was revealed Rothstein was a money-lender to most of the nation's top gangsters and had bankrolled many of this nation's top illegal schemes.

Grey Lag is remembered today by the New York handicap race that bears his name. Sporting Blood's name is among the historic roster of Travers' winners, while Prudery, the great Whitney mare, has been forgotten.

ૐ

16

ONE FOR SARATOGA

ﾐ

When Lincoln Kirstein and George Balanchine announced in 1966 that they planned to bring the New York City Ballet to the new Performing Arts Center in the tiny upstate community of Saratoga Springs, critics scoffed and board members resisted.

Opposition softened, from the inside. Governor Nelson Rockefeller, who had spearheaded the building of the 5,000 seat amphitheatre and its sloping lawns to hold another 20,000 or more, put pressure on from his enormous arsenal of corporate boards and state commissions, and soon Saratoga was the place to go.

Balanchine told the sophisticated New York dance critics he would educate an audience in Saratoga, teach them about dance, and build a loyal support base for his troupe. He did just that.

Balanchine arranged programs that featured the well-known ballets "Swan Lake," the "Nutcracker," and his wonderful production of a three-part series joined for a full evening of ballet, "Jewels." Saratoga audiences grew in size and sophistication, and Balanchine was hailed for making what had been an art form without an audience in America—ballet—entertainment for an ever-growing number of supporters.

His company was very healthy. It had a new home at Lincoln Center in New York, a new summer home at Saratoga, and a waiting list of places to travel. The old Russian master had achieved success with his dance company.

For many years there had been pressure on Balanchine to choreograph the ballet of his youth in Russia, "Coppelia," but he had always resisted. "It is not time," the most famous choreographer of the 20th century would say, "I am not ready."

Balanchine had grown up with "Coppelia," which had been done by Marius Petipa and premiered in St. Petersburg, Russia, in 1884. Through the years, the story of the doll who had come to life, based on the 1815 story "Der Sandmann," by E.T.A. Hoffmann, became one of the great "story line" ballets.

Most of the top Russian ballerinas had at one time in their careers been seen in the lead Swanilda. The dancer most considered the best in the role was Alexandra Danilova.

During the early 1970s, after the New York City Ballet had become well established in its summer home, Balanchine started talking about "... doing something special for Saratoga." He had been welcomed warmly to the social scene in Saratoga, most of his company felt very much at home in the Spa city, and many had purchased homes, the only real "home" many of the dancers had ever known.

He was sitting backstage one morning in July 1973, following the master classes and morning rehearsals and he commented: "It is time I did something just for Saratoga, something for the children, something for our loyal summer audience. Perhaps now, Coppelia."

Those around him, who knew him best, were shocked. After decades of trying to get him to do a new version of the classic Russian ballet, he was going to do it for the unsophisticated upstate audience who, the New Yorkers felt, would not be able to appreciate it.

Balanchine further shocked the insiders as he brought Madame Danilova to the company. The old woman worked tirelessly with the younger woman most considered the best American dancer of the day, Patricia McBride, to bring alive the classic role of Swanilda, as Danilova had danced it many years before in Russia. Danilova also worked on creating the costumes, designing the sets, creating the scene of the ballet as she had known it in her younger days on the Russian stage.

Balanchine then sent more shock waves through the nest of observers watching the development of the long-awaited ballet. Instead of choosing one of the classically trained Scandinavian or Russian dancers from his impressive stable, he announced the meaty role of Dr. Coppelius would go to the company's long-time character actor/dancer/mime, the Brooklyn-born Shaun

O'Brien. Balanchine had long been promising O'Brien that one day he would write a role for him, but no one ever believed it would be something as big and important as Dr. Coppelius.

Madame Danilova and Balanchine worked for months on the new ballet. Sets, costumes, lighting, and endless re-writing honed the work, which was finally given its world premiere on the SPAC stage on July 17, 1974. The curtain went up just a bit after the scheduled 8:15, and two hours later, the huge Saratoga audience that had filled the seats and the lawns to thank Balanchine, and the doubting New York writers finally agreed. This was a hit. The experts and the summer audience knew they had seen a moment of greatness and the creation of a dance classic.

Shaun O'Brien was a star, and Patricia McBride had grown even more in stature for her performance as the doll who came to life. Everyone had expected the great skills McBride brought to the roll, but no one, not Balanchine and probably not even O'Brien himself, expected the towering performance the long-time character actor brought to the role of Doctor Coppelius.

O'Brien created a sense of gentleness, pride, and a new feeling of love into the role that had previously been seen as a part for a tottering, fumbling old fool.

O'Brien is one of the cast members who had bought a home in Saratoga. He and show business photographer Christopher Alexander had purchased an old, run-down victorian on Greenfield Avenue and restored it.

A quiet, unassuming and long-time member of the company, O'Brien had followed his sister to dancing lessons in the Bay Ridge section of Brooklyn. "She became a nun, and I became a dancer," he laughs in telling the story of how he ended up on the Saratoga stage. Following the first performance, O'Brien didn't even come out for the final curtain call of the premiere. His work was done in the second act, so he had gotten dressed.

In subsequent performances, he learned to stay around and take the standing cheers of audiences who recognized his outstanding work. Years later, as O'Brien danced his "farewell" performance at Saratoga, a revival of "Coppelia," he returned to the middle of the big stage alone, as thousands stood to cheer and say goodbye to a dancer/actor/mime who had won their hearts with his characterization of Dr. Coppelius.

Everyone knew Balanchine had a major hit with "Coppelia." It was mounted in New York the next season, playing to sell-out crowds, and remains one of the major ballets in active repertory for the company. "I had promised something very special for Saratoga," Balanchine told a packed press conference the day after the premiere. "Coppelia will always be remembered as Saratoga's ballet."

The opening night cast will also always remember the premiere of "Coppelia," for another reason. To mark the world premiere of this important work, a big celebration party was held backstage following the show. Dancers, stage crews, major supporters and a young writer joined SPAC officials for the party in the large rehearsal hall. Next day, more than half the cast, stagehands, board members, and the writer were felled by food poisoning. A caterer had left mounds of chicken salad by open windows, and a warm breeze had done its work.

The second performance of "Coppelia" featured many of the women dancers dressed as men and others doing parts they had only seen done the night before. The show must go on, they say, and it did, but it was a struggle for two nights.

O'Brien called to ask if I were still alive. "Barely," I noted. "We shall always have something to remember from the premiere of 'Coppelia,' " the Irish leprechaun laughed. It took some time for him to realize what he had to remember from that night was not food poisoning, but that he had become a major dance star.

ॐ

17

BASEBALL

ぇ

For many years, Glens Falls was best known in sporting circles as the host site of the Eastern States Basketball Tournament. This was a showcase for the best basketball talent in the east coast's best prep school and the Catholic high schools.

There has also long been the mistaken impression that "Glen Falls, isn't that where they have the car race?" has been asked many times. "It's *Glens* Falls, the car race is in Watkins Glen," is the correct answer. Emphasize the "Glens."

But really, Glens Falls has long been a baseball town. When you ventured to the playing fields of Crandall Park as a lad, playing baseball the right way, without a uniform and with only the number of kids who showed up—usually not 18—until it got so dark you couldn't see the taped-up baseball, you were fed stories of the Glens Falls Clerks.

The Clerks were the pre-war team in Glens Falls. Over the years, stories of their skills have become larger than life. They could throw harder, hit further, and run faster than any group of players ever assembled, if you listen to the great stories. The one most heard, and sworn to by scores of Clerk loyalists, was Roy Akins poling a long home run that landed in Glen Street, bounced and broke the window in the filling station across the street from Crandall Park.

There is no question the Clerks were talented, and they had several players on the roster who later popped up in the major leagues. College players played during the summer, and the Clerks were the only game in town. There was no television, no

Northway to the Expos in Montreal, or the Yankees and the Mets in New York.

But the teams of post-war vintage are those more remembered now. The Doblers and the famed Glens Falls Independents. The Doblers had more raw talent, the Independents played better baseball, and that was because of the squat catcher/manager/GM/owner Wady Rozelle.

If baseball had not yet been invented when Wady Rozelle was around, someone would have thought it up and made him a catcher. He was Birdie Tebbitts, Yogi Berra, and Johnny Bench rolled into one. He was made to squat behind the plate and pick foul tips off the bats of opponent hitters. He could throw line drives to second base, and controlled the bat when he was at the plate himself.

Spending a Sunday afternoon at Crandall Park, sitting in the cool shade of the towering pines watching the Indies and the Doblers play a pair of games is a baseball memory that will last forever.

Between games, the players would go back into the picnic area behind the ball field and eat with their families, then go back to play the seven-inning nightcap. Like Wrigley Field, there were no lights at Crandall Park.

But unlike Wrigley Field, they could not charge you to watch a game. The story was that old Henry Crandall had noted in his will that no admission could be charged at his park. To help pay for the baseballs and the umpires, card tables were set up at the entry at both ends of the bleachers that stretched from behind first base, around the back of home plate and up the line to third base. Someone from the teams would sit there with an open cigar box and when you entered, it was expected that you would drop a donation into the box. You could always climb up the back of the bleachers to get a seat, so the guy at the tables wouldn't give you a dirty look for not tossing anything into the kitty.

Young kids always sat on the top rows of the bleachers so they could jump off and chase foul balls that sailed back into the pines. There were some tough scrambles for the foul balls, because when you brought the ball back to the guy at the card table he gave you a dime for it. Big money for an 11 year old, especially if you could get two or three during the afternoon.

The Independents had been around a long time. Wady Rozelle had been catching for years, and his team had some outstanding players. Pete Smith held down third, later first base, and a skinny guy named Art LaRock was a vacuum cleaner around second. Bud Morrison played first base for many seasons, and his long hits were legends.

A variety of players moved through the Indy lineup, but the regulars were always there. Bo Bolster was the business manager, he ran the card tables and worked on the schedules. There was usually a seven-inning game on Tuesday nights and weekend doubleheaders.

The Doblers and the Hudson Falls Greenjackets were always part of the loyal opposition, and other teams drifted in and out of the semi-pro league. St. Johnsville always had good teams, and there was a trip or two each season to Vermont.

Lefty Storey was one of the top Indy pitchers for years and as young high school players came of age, they moved to the mound for the Glens Falls squad.

Each summer, some of the fabled traveling teams would visit Glens Falls and do battle with the Independents. The House of David, with its bearded players, were regular visitors. One season, the Brooklyn Dodgers had a road team of young players, "Future Dodger Stars," and the game was played at Glens Falls High School's diamond on Sherman Avenue so the teams could charge admission.

The Doblers also had some outstanding hitters. Johnny Marcantonio always brought all the picnickers to the edge of the woods when he hit because there was always the chance he would "park" one in the deepest parts of the endless outfield. His smooth swing would cause the ball to jump off the bat and start to rise, something that only happens when real hitters cause a short piece of wood to come in contact with a baseball.

The Doblers also had several good pitchers over the years. On a hot Sunday afternoon one of them, Willard Hunter, star of Glens Falls High School, was pitching and scouts from the big leagues sat around in the bleachers looking on. Willy had a man on first, something that always gave him problems; he was a thrower not a stylist. The runner went, and catcher Byron Lapham threw a strike toward second base. Willy didn't duck, he just turned his head to watch, and the throw caught him right in back of the ear. The big lefthander went down in a heap on the mound, and Lapham thought he had killed him.

They carried him into the field house and put his head under the cold water of the drinking fountain. As he came to, he recognized his worried catcher, and asked about the runner, "Was he out?" The Brooklyn Dodgers recognized Willy Hunter's talent and also heard he was punting for the Glens Falls football team. They quickly moved his education to Petty Prep, where he did not play football.

Hunter's regular catcher was a talented, lanky kid from Hudson Falls, Yogi Young. His mechanics behind the plate were wonderful to watch, and he seemed a sure bet to go on to pro baseball, but education got in the way, as he went to college and returned here to coach for many years.

A wonderful baseball trivia question: Who was the last pitcher to win a doubleheader in the National League? Willy Hunter won both ends of a twinbill one Sunday afternoon for the New York Mets, pitching relief in both games and getting the victories.

While semi-pro baseball was the major leagues of Glens Falls, young people learned the sport by playing in the Saturday Morning League, which was sponsored by the *Glens Falls Times* and did not play on Saturdays, but nearly every other morning both at Crandall Park and East Field. When you got to be 16, you moved to the Neighborhood League, which played in the evenings also at Rec Field and East. High school baseball had a short season, and most of the real baseball was played in the recreation leagues during the summer.

Television, the Northway, and Little League, having eight year olds play in uniforms with umpires, all changed baseball. The semi-pro teams folded for lack of support and players, and on Sunday's, except for an occasional American Legion game, Crandall Park's diamond is empty, the gas station across Glen Street has been torn down, and kids can't make a dime on foul balls any more.

≈

18

THE BOSS

%

Today there is little thought of mob crime and family-ruling dons running the rackets in the North Country. There are a few "wise guys" dumped on the Northway from time to time, and 50 years ago Walter Winchell wrote, "If you want to commit murder go to Warren County."

There was a time, however, when the North Country had its own "Don" who ran the illegal booze business with an iron hand until he was finally brought down by an elaborate federal program.

"The rackets boss of the North Country in New York during and after the 1920s was a short, medium-built, well-dressed, quick-thinking American known as "The Doc." Born in Saratoga Springs in 1904, he did not reach beyond five feet, five inches in stature, but rose to be top man over the rest of his underworld contemporaries.

"From an office used as a headquarters in the village of his birth, he bossed the area from the Mohawk River north to the Canadian boundary. He moved in sporty circles, ruled with a firm hand, and had a way of getting things done."

So begins chapter XVI in the narrative book entitled *Illicit Alcohol*, written in 1965 by a long time member of the Treasury Department's Alcohol Tax branch, James A. Donohue.

The report, dedicated to the late Attorney General Robert Kennedy, never gained much attention, but it makes for fascinating reading by anyone interested in the comings and goings of gangsters who controlled the upstate area during the period from the late 1920s to the beginning of World War II.

Donohue, a native of Watervliet, was sent to this area to observe the workings of the crime gangs, mostly those who made their money from selling illicit alcohol. This was not during the times of prohibition, when local police used to shoot it out on Glen Street with bootleggers making the run from Canada to Albany and New York. This was when it was still profitable to sell untaxed alcohol, making use of all the stills, trucks, and unemployed available during this time of depression to make, run, and sell the illegal hooch.

Donohue was no Elliott Ness. Getting his name in the headlines for making arrests was not his job or his style. He was a quiet observer, working mostly undercover, to observe and make cases against the Depression bootleggers.

He must have kept copious notes, because his book is filled with details, many of them from his work in New York City, but quite a bit from the time he spent in the Saratoga Springs-Glens Falls-Minerva area.

Writing about "Saratoga's Doc" he wrote: "One of Doc's major sources of income was derived from the illicit manufacture of alcohol, commonly referred to as 'alki' or 'white' in bootleg circles.

"After a short respite in the alcohol manufacturing business during early 1939, the Doc gathered his oldtime still managers and announced the intention of running again. Joe the Fox, Louis the Torpedo, alias Dynamite, and Harry the Jew began to see more of each other during the days that followed in the summer and autumn of 1939."

Donohue, like most good undercover cops, was a loner. He spent weeks following and watching those he was investigating, developing an ironclad case that required no informers, no one copping a plea and no civilian witnesses that could suddenly change their story on the witness stand.

"This sort of case stands completely on the evidence gathered by the agent," he wrote. "Regardless of the subsequent attitude of other witnesses, it gets results. This system will work anytime, anywhere."

Donohue was sent to try his method of operation on the famed "Saratoga Doc," a kingpin the feds had tried to topple time and time again with no results.

"There were no informers available," Donohue wrote in his journal. He pointed out that some "wise guy" hijackers had once tried to hoist some of Doc's wares and when word got around of their fate, "no one ever tried it again." There was never an official account of what happened to them, but unofficial stories were quite gruesome.

The Doc's group used to hold target practice in the cellar of the old United States Hotel in Saratoga after the place was closed following the end of racing season. Sonny Boy was their champion marksman by a wide margin. The group held competition that consisted of shooting at the most difficult of moving targets, rats running across the cellar floor.

Donohue watched and waited and wrote in his notebooks. He also spent some time doing some target practice of his own, "...rats not being difficult to find, but very difficult to hit," he wrote.

The federal agent developed information the group hung out in the Chicago Club. His observations disclosed they had dismantled still equipment stored at Shady Acres Farm nine miles north of Saratoga. They put the still, several hundred drums of molasses and other supplies for making alcohol in a large warehouse at the corner of Ash and Franklin streets in Saratoga.

"This material was left over from a big plant we broke up about a year earlier at South Glens Falls," Donohue noted. "Racketeers from New York City were the principal defendants in that case."

Donohue slipped into Saratoga Springs early on the morning of July 8, 1939, and started a long investigation that was to ultimately lead to the break-up of Doc and his Saratoga Gang.

The officer watched them gather regularly at the Chicago Club on the west side of Woodlawn Avenue, just north of the Division Street corner. He soon learned about Shady Acres Farm off the Old Glens Falls Road at Wilton. Donohue learned the group regularly went north on Route 9 to some place called Minerva.

He would station himself, he wrote, "at the bridge across the Hudson River at Glens Falls," to watch for them going north. "The bridge was a bottleneck for traffic moving from points south to the country further north," he correctly noted, and he spent considerable time on the bridge carefully noting the gang's travels north.

He had other agents trace the destination of the gang's truck as it made frequent trips to an abandoned farm near Minerva. For weeks, the agents watched from a distance as the Saratoga group built a massive still on the property deep in the Adirondacks.

Construction of the still stopped suddenly, and the agents feared they had been spotted, but they learned from a local workman on the project that it had been abandoned because it was discovered there was not a good supply of water on the property and the alcohol operation had to be relocated.

Under cover of night, and under the watchful eye of Donohue and his partners, the entire operation was "secretly" moved to a pig farm on the Petrified Gardens Road in Saratoga. Agents watched as the gang members labored to re-build the still and then construct a dam across a stream on the property. Soon a water supply was available that could fill four round wooden vats that held 5,500 gallons each. It was to be a truly massive alcohol manufacturing operation, one the Treasury Department later said would have been the largest to their knowledge in the Upstate area.

On November 2, 1939, federal agents raided the farm, rounded up the entire group, and closed the huge still before it produced its first gallon of illicit and untaxed alcohol.

Saratoga's Doc went on trial in Federal Court at Malone, New York on July 17, 1940. During the trial, one of the jurors told the presiding federal judge that another member of the jury had taken money from the gang to hold out for a not-guilty verdict. The defendants were secretly charged with jury tampering, the juror quietly changed, and on August 2, 1940, the Saratoga Gang and its leader were convicted of conspiracy to operate illicit distilleries and sent to federal prison.

The Doc later entered a guilty plea to jury tampering, getting him an additional three years in prison.

Federal officers said the conviction of the Saratoga Doc was the end of an era of illicit alcohol manufacturing in the Saratoga-Glens Falls area. The feds will privately tell you that several of the group later moved into the beer business.

ஐ

19

ARE YOU SURE THE NEXT TIME'S BY FIRE?

ঽ৶

When our group was growing up, we raised floods to an art form. It seemed there was a program among our gang to find new and innovative ways to make water flow into our cellar.

Over the years we had floods from diapers being in the toilet, floods when the tiny part deep inside the washing machine that shuts off the water when the tub has filled didn't, floods when the rain overwhelmed the storm sewers, flooded the street and forced its way past the "guaranteed" trap the plumber put into the pipe the washing machine empties into, and boiled up the pipe and into the cellar.

We had a flood when the hot water tank ruptured, floods when the automatic foolproof shutoff valve in the dehumidifier got fooled, and water poured out of the very full collection pail. There was a flood when rain poured into the cellar window well and found its way to the ski rack. We had a flood when the ice on the eaves made the melting snow back up, come through the roof, find its way into a hot air duct and drip out onto the piano for a day or two, until someone noticed the keys looked a bit wet.

Some of these are once-in-a-while floods. Some are too-often occurring floods, like the one from the rain in the street. It was decided the best thing to do with the guilty pipe into which the hose from the washing machine goes in normal times and where water from the storm sewers gushes out in bad times was to thread it and when it rained, screw down a cap. Then, the plumber explained, when it rains, and the "guaranteed" trap doesn't work, the water won't be able to get out of the pipe, onto the floor, and into all the things you always think will only be sitting in the cellar for a short time.

All you have to do, is when it rains go down into the cellar, take the hose from the washing machine out of the pipe, and screw on the cap. It works very well, unless you are in a hurry the next time you go into the cellar with a load of clothes and turn on the washing machine with the hose still out of the pipe. This happened so many times we now nearly always unplug the washing machine and tie the electric cord to the hose. Another almost-perfect solution.

One Saturday, during a major, major storm, not one member of our large group was home. No one was there to take out the hose and put on the cap. So when the rain filled the street, water filled the cellar. When someone went downstairs about midnight to wash a uniform for the next morning's waitress work, the latest attempt to create an indoor pool was discovered.

When great amounts of water fill the cellar, like when the part failed or the ice melted, then you can call the friendly firemen to come and pump out your basement. But, when there is about half an inch of water on half of the floor, you mop, blot, and if it is not a Sunday morning, rent a water vacuum.

So, on this Sunday morning it was mop and blot. Someone, probably getting ready to return to college, had tossed two blankets onto the floor in front of the washer. Do you know how much water two blankets soak up overnight? Lots! Olympic weight lifters train on such items.

So as some of the boys mopped and blotted, I decided the best route for the blankets was to take them to a laundromat rather than putting them in our overworked machine and probably risk making the washing machine repair man less lonely.

Being in a commercial laundromat on a Sunday morning was a new experience for me. I found this large washing machine that looked like it would handle the blankets with ease, but discovered it ate quarters like a Las Vegas slot machine. "Insert eight quarters," the magic marker note on the machine ordered. Another machine, this one on the back wall, took my dollars and gave back quarters. Better than a slot machine, it paid off every time. Well, nearly every time, I discovered.

The wet blankets in, the eight quarters in, "pour in soap powder" the light told me. I didn't know it meant just a little soap powder.

The suds were starting to come out the little door on the top when I saw the button marked "push and hold for 30 seconds for high suds." I pushed, and held for a couple minutes and finally the suds went down.

On "final rinse," there was still a lot of soap in the water, so I figured I would put the blankets through again, using the entire cycle as a rinse. But, having no more quarters and no more dollars, I drove to the supermarket a few blocks away and got some cash from the Shop and Bank, handy to have that card.

Back to the laundromat just in time to see a little girl climb into a dryer. Her brother was slamming the door when someone yelled at them to stop playing with the dryers, and she climbed out. He got in. They must be regulars.

Two dollars into the bill changer, eight quarters into the machine, nothing happens. "You must have used a Canadian quarter," the irritated manager says. "If I did I got it from your stupid change machine," I tell him.

It was a Canadian quarter, he found it after he had taken the machine apart. He found five of them, along with a handful of U.S.A. quarters in the long throat of the slot.

The machine started up. I left and went to the car wash to pass the time. Returning, the nice lady who had yelled at the kids playing in the dryer was folding clothes. She looked up and said: "The manager noticed you forgot to put in soap powder, so he put some in for you. It looks like he put too much though, all you men put too much soap in washing machines."

The suds were everywhere again. I held the button down. The light said final rinse, there was more soap in the rinse than anyone uses in wash.

An hour later I got the blankets home, not dried, but certainly washed and finally rinsed.

The boys had finished mopping and blotting the water. The cellar was clean and dry once again, patiently awaiting its next flood experience.

When I heard the washing machine going, I knew. Even before the middle girl smiled and said, "Don't worry about my blankets, I tossed them in the machine."

❧

20

RIDING TO GLORY

ﻉﻪ

Over the years there have been several fine athletes come out of the Glens Falls/Saratoga/North Country area. We have done quite well in baseball, skiing, bobsledding, running, basketball, and football.

While several of our athletes have made it to the professional level, not many have become full-fledged world champions. Although the term "world champion" has been tossed around quite liberally in recent years by television commentators, the sports pages, and especially fight promoters, to be a real champion of all the world in your sport is quite an achievement.

A Glens Falls native who made it to that level was a bicycle rider named Harry D. Elkes. Much of his story has been forgotten since bicycle riding faded from popularity for decades. It has now returned, not only for those who ride long distances, but as part of triathlons and in short road races.

Elkes lived in Glens Falls with his parents and a sister. His father, "Pop" Elkes, was a well-known bicycle rider, and he passed the skills and the love of the sport along to his son Harry.

The lad was only 16 when he rode as an amateur cyclist in 1895. He did so well in the competition with older riders, that he turned professional a year later. In 1898, he became the sensation of the bike tracks.

At the time, bicycle racing was a major professional sport. Elke's feats on the pro tracks of the day were quite remarkable, since he was racing against men much older and a great deal more experienced.

In 1898, he defeated all the major pro bike riders of the world and set several world records behind pace. It was in vogue at that time to have bicycles paced by a motor-driven machine, usually a large motorcycle.

During the 1899 season, Elkes won every major event in the United States and Europe, and was proclaimed the champion pro bike rider of the world.

He was a participant in the famed six-day bicycle race at the Charles River in Boston, and that introduced him to the best riders from France, England, and throughout America. He established a new mark for 25 miles and he set a new world record for the hour, which further added to his title as "champion of the world."

The 1901 National Paced Championship was held in Buffalo. The 22-year old from Glens Falls challenged the nation's best riders and won handily. It seemed Elkes would win every race he entered. Then he was injured during the 1902 season and did not finish the schedule of major competition or compete in the nationals.

Friends reported he considered retiring. He spent several months at home in Glens Falls. He discussed the possibility of leaving the sport with his family and friends, but decided against it and was soon working out to regain his strength and skills on the racing bicycle.

He became engaged to Edith Garrett of Glens Falls, daughter of Dr. and Mrs. J.S. Garrett. Dr. Garrett was the first of generations of Garrett's who practiced dentistry in Glens Falls.

Elkes announced his engagement, and also said 1903 would be his final year of professional competition on the bike track. Following the season, he would retire at the ripe old age of 24 and study medicine with his long-time friend Dr. F.H. Chase of Chelsea, Massachusetts. He would then marry Miss Garrett and open a practice of family medicine, probably in his home town of Glens Falls.

Those who knew the young athlete were unanimous in their praise of him. They admired not only his athletic ability and his enormous skills on the racing bike, but also admired his sportsmanship and his willingness to help others, even competitors.

The young couple planned a June wedding in Glens Falls, and it was with high hopes for the future that Elkes left his home village in late May to take part in the Boston Memorial Day bicycle events in Charles River Park, the bike track that had propelled him to national fame.

The 20-mile motor-paced race was the highlight of the day, and Elkes gave the large crowd quite a show. As he passed the 10-mile mark, well in front, it was announced he had set a new world record for that distance. A similar announcement was made as he he passed the 15-mile mark. A new record for the 20 miles seemed assured.

Because of the quality of the competition Elkes brought to the event, there were only three riders taking part. The two riders considered the second and third best in the nation, Bobby Walthous and Will C. Stinson, were the only cyclists to challenge Elkes.

Elkes came pounding around on the 16th mile when the chain on his racing bike broke. Showing his experience and sportsmanship, Elkes coasted into the backstretch and moved to the side to get out of the way of the two riders following him.

Suddenly the loose chain caught in the wheel and Elkes was thrown out onto the track. At that moment the big motorcycle ridden by F.A. Gately, which was pacing Stinson, shot around the turn.

Gately had only an instant to see the helpless Elkes sprawled on the track. He tried to turn the speeding motorcycle to avoid the fallen rider, but could not. The motorcycle slammed into Elkes, sending Gately and his peddler Stinson to the track in a mass of machines and bodies.

A Boston reporter at the scene wrote: "Women fainted, men groaned in agony, and a panic started in the grandstand."

Gately's motorcycle was going at a high rate of speed when it struck Elkes. The impact broke the young champion's neck, crushed his body, and broke most of his bones. He died in an ambulance en route to a nearby hospital.

Stinson suffered three major head injuries, his face was bruised, and the skin was torn from the entire front of his body. Gately lost a foot, which was crushed, and had a spine injury.

The frightening accident, one of the most horrible ever witnessed at a sporting event, is credited with being a major cause of motor-paced bicycle racing losing popularity as a major national sport.

Elkes, who had won the six-day bicycle race in Madison Square Garden and gained international fame for his riding feats at the Paris Exposition, was brought home to Glens Falls for services. The First Baptist Church on Maple Street was filled to overflowing. The Rev. William O. Stearns officiated assisted by the Rev. George L. Richardson. The entire community mourned the death of this brilliant young athlete who was just on the verge of beginning his life as a husband and doctor.

Elkes is buried in Glens Falls Cemetery on Bay Street. His grave is easy to find. His headstone is not topped with an angel, nor a cross, but with the carving of a bicycle wheel.

❧

21

THE WITCH

Ted Kaufmann used to work in New York City as an advertising executive. When he decided to go straight, he moved to the Adirondacks to become a witch.

The "Hebrew Leprechaun" as he likes to bill himself, is the North Country's most famous dowser or water witch. He is called on regularly to find where to drill a well on a building site and loves to challenge doubters by having them use a forked stick to seek out water.

Kaufmann is perfect for the part. A gnarley little man, he seems a bit mysterious, and after many years waving a dowsing rod at the world, knows how to play his role with tremendous effectiveness.

Once during a talk sponsored by the Lake George Historical Association at the old Warren County Court House, he talked about vibes of old defendants, of the fact that the first man ever sent to the electric chair in New York was, "convicted in this room," and then "found" water as he walked across the old floor holding a dead stick from a cherry tree high above his head.

The stick quivered, then snapped down to point at the floor. "There is a vein of water under the building, right here," he declared. Titters of laughter swept the room until he asked an engineer there for just this reason, "Is there any water flowing under this building?"

"Yes," the engineer said, consulting his drawings, and told the crowd, "there is an old stream that flows to the lake, and it crosses under the building right there," he said pointing at a point floor at which Kaufmann's cherry twig had pointed moments before.

Kaufmann loves the doubters, they fill the rooms when he speaks and ask the same questions over and over, ones for which he usually has an answer. "Magic, there is no magic in dowsing," he says. "Anyone can do it with practice. Sensitivity is within the person. You must work to bring it out. I am not a psychic, I cannot see the future. I do use ESP (extrasensory perception), but everyone has that, we just don't use it."

As usual someone asked, "Don't you have to use a live branch from an apple tree to find water?" Laughing, Kaufmann dowses the floor, having a wire coat hanger, a piece of plastic, two metal rods and a Russian dowsing wand all bend or swing together at the point the engineer has said there was water.

A young boy comes into the room with his parents, they are late for the talk, and Kaufmann watches for such folks. "Young man," he says to the boy, "do you know what dowsing is all about?" The lad smiles and says he thinks it's something about finding water with a stick.

Kaufmann hands him the cherry branch, tells him how to hold it and has him walk slowly across the room. At the exact spot, the stick snaps down to the floor, the crowd reacts, Kaufmann laughs. He has the boy's father try it. The stick quivers at the spot. "This is nonsense," the older man says.

"Concentrate, don't doubt it," the witch tells him and when he tries again, the stick snaps down.

Finding water with a stick is nothing new. People have been dowsing for centuries and not always for water. John D. Rockefeller had petroleum dowsers called "doodlebugs," and one of them is credited with finding the first major Rockefeller well. Dowsing sticks hang all over the walls in rooms at the Rockefeller home in Terrytown. Kaufmann notes Alfred Einstein was a dowser, so was Thomas A. Edison.

While Kaufmann has lots of fun with his talks and appearances at a variety of shows about seeking water, he does not talk about many of the other things he has been called on to do with his dowsing wand.

He agrees with scientists who believe there is a logical explanation for the divining rod dipping toward water because some field of electrical waves, hertzian waves, that cause changes in terrestrial magnetism due to the underground water sources. He explains the reason a plummet attached to a key chain held over a man's hand will swing back and forth and held over a woman's hand will swing in little circles is because of the electrical energy that flows off your hand according to your sex. You can doubt it, but if you try it, be ready.

He can map dowse, but won't for public shows. Police called on him to try and find two men who had been lost in Lake George when their pickup truck had apparently gone through the ice somewhere out on the lake. He refuses to talk about it, but amazed cops, who had searched for weeks, locating the truck and its drowned driver and soon after the passenger, deep in the lake. They won't publicly say they got the information from Kaufmann and his swinging plummet, but they did.

There was a happier ending for the two canoeists who got dumped in the Upper Hudson River several years ago and had their overturned boat go tossing down the white water river for miles. Cops got a "fix" from the witch, hiked in, and brought the two chilled paddlers out of the woods. No, they never told them, because the witch wants that kind of information kept quiet. "Every kook in the north woods would be after me, all I do is find water," he comments.

Gore Mountain Ski Center can vouch for that. They had a big problem in finding a water source for an enlarged snowmaking system. "And I don't even ski anymore," he laughs, confirming he did make a major water find for the ski area.

Dowsing is an ancient art. There are cave drawings of a dowser at work in the Atlas Mountains of North Africa and the pictures have been carbon dated to be 8,000 years old. Dowsing was described by Cicero and Tacitus, used by the Cornish muses, and in the days of Queen Elizabeth. There are those who will tell you Moses was dowsing when he tapped that rock.

Does Kaufmann play the role well? He lives in an Adirondack hideaway he has dubbed, "Bewilderness, NY," a spot somewhere near North River. Is it really a place? "I get my mail," he laughs.

One day after he had map dowsed the location of my house without having the slightest idea where it was, I asked to try the stick. He walked around a large field, the stick bent at a point he marked on the ground. He gave me the stick, tied a blindfold over my eyes and shoved me off into the field. I did, I swear to you, I did feel the stick bend. I took off the blindfold. You know where I was standing.

"Don't worry," he answered the concerned look on my face, "there's always a logical explanation."

ॐ

22

THE MOHICAN MARKET

ત&

Everyone used to come to the "Falls" to shop. It mattered not if you lived in Lake George or Corinth or Moreau, you made regular visits to Glens Falls for serious shopping.

Many in Vermont and Northern Warren County still plan shopping trips "to Glens Falls," when they visit the stores of neighboring Queensbury. Old habits, and terms, are tough to lose.

While holiday shopping trips were to find gifts in the great variety of stores in the area, the regular shopping trips were for food. During the week you could pick up a loaf of bread, a pound of bologna, and a quart of milk —unless the milkman left it at your door every other day— at the corner store where you lived. But those basket-crushing trips to load up on food for breakfasts —everyone ate a big breakfast, lunch —kids came home, they didn't stay at school, and suppers —only rich people ate dinner— were made to the supermarkets in Glens Falls.

To the Grand Unions, one on Glen Street where now Washington Street creates an intersection, and one on Ridge Street where now there is a drug store. There were several Central Markets, they are now Price Choppers. There was a major supermarket on Glen Street in Monument Square, another on Warren Street where Lazarus now holds forth, and one at the foot of Glen Street Hill. The A&P was on South Street next to Glens Falls Diner, an area that is now only parking. No matter how you entered Glens Falls, a supermarket awaited your food dollars.

While most of those stores were used by city residents and shoppers from surrounding communities alike, there was one unique store that was pretty much directed at Glens Falls folks. The Mohican Market on Warren Street had its own personality and was quite unlike any of the other more modern, busy stores.

As you entered the Mohican, a meat case that went all the way down the west wall greeted you. It was filled with all kinds of great red meat, as well as chickens, turkeys, ducks, salads, baked beans, cold cuts, hot dogs, salt pork, bacon, and a seemingly endless variety of meats. Standing behind this store-long case were "meatmen." They wore blood-stained white aprons, most had on a cap with a pencil over one ear, some still wore cuffs of straw. The floor behind the meat case was covered with sawdust to catch the dripping blood and fat, and huge meat blocks held an endless number and variety of knives, cleavers, and other instruments to cut, wrap, roll, debone or otherwise prepare the meat for the customers.

Snap Owens and his crew, which sometimes included my grand-pere, Henry C. Metivier, were there to answer questions, make suggestions, and most importantly help the shopping housewife get meat for the week. Having company? Grand-pere or one of his colleagues would cut, tie, and wrap a crown roast. Roasting chickens were prepared for Sunday dinner, and piles of cold meat were cut and wrapped for lunches.

The meatmen knew most of their customers, knew what the husbands did or did not like, and realized the economic status of the family created the number of hot dogs in a pound. I made the mistake of asking my grandfather one day why some people got 12 franks in a pound and others the usual nine. What he explained to me is now called foodstamps, and costs us more to administer than the meatmen knowing to give a family a few extra hot dogs.

Want a few pounds of hamburger for a meat loaf? It was ground right in front of you. Huge pieces of chuck tossed into the stainless steel hopper on top of an old red grinder. The meatman would tamp it down with a wooden dowel, and catch the fresh ground beef in a stiff paper butter dish as it poured out the release on the side of the grinder. Pork, veal, beef, it all went through the grinder during the day. Each evening the machine would be scoured in scalding hot water and left to air until the next morning.

Want some steaks? How thick, how many and what kind, sirloin, porterhouse, T-bone, filet, bottom or top round cubed? They were cut to your order from loins sitting in the case with "U.S. Govt. Inspected" purple stamp marks along the fat.

How about a roast? That caused a consultation about the number of people coming to the table, what kind of cut would be best for a potroast or an oven roast, how the finances were that week, and if the cook was a veteran who knew how to soften up some tough cut, or a beginner who needed all the help tender cuts could provide.

Want chicken? You bought a chicken, a whole chicken. No one knew you could sell parts. If you wanted it cut up, they did it. They didn't chop it, they cut it. "Never hit a chicken with a cleaver," I learned as soon as I was old enough to sit in the backroom and pick pinfeathers, "it shatters the bones." I knew if I ever saw someone swinging a cleaver at a chicken, he was a clerk, not a meatman.

Once the meat was cut or ground, it was wrapped in a package of brown paper and tied with a string that came down near the wrapping table from a huge spool near the ceiling. Every meatman knew how to tuck in the ends of the paper, swing the string around and secure the package, its price written on the side in pencil.

On the other side of the Mohican was the fish counter, watched over by one-eyed Joe Nolan. "You never know if he or the fish is looking at you," was my grand-pere's favorite line about his friend and neighbor Joe.

The fish counter smelled like a fish counter, as dozens of varieties of fish were placed out in view. Sitting on crushed ice the ice man brought into the store in great wooden tubs each morning, the fish were fresh, well cleaned, and came with an explanation of the best way to cook them to any young wife seeking to get better in her kitchen.

Shellfish like clams, scallops, crabs, and mussels were on the ice or in bags. Oysters were dipped into a bucket from a large white crock and the lobsters swam in big tanks, their claws held shut by red rubber bands.

Friday was fish day then, and the lines were long, as most of the East End got the food necessary to go to heaven because eating meat on Friday was not the way.

There was a very special place in the Mohican. During the holidays, nearly everyone baked fruitcakes, and at Easter, fruit-filled hotcross buns. That meant having to purchase glazed fruit, and the Mohican had stone crocks of all kinds of glazed fruit. Red and green cherries, raisins, all kinds of things needed to make your fruit cake as much like the one Charley Garland baked at the Queen City Bakery as possible.

Want pasta? Every type of spaghetti, noodle and macaroni was available. Loose in boxes, baskets, and bins, you purchased as much as you needed.

My favorite part of the Mohican was the bakery. Everything, and that meant rolls, bread, cakes, donuts, eclairs, cream puffs, all the offerings were baked in the Mohican kitchens. Each August, my grand-mere would order a special cake for my birthday. The bakers would trim it with huge roses made from rich icing, and my friends would battle to get one of the pieces covered with a bright red or yellow sugar rose.

When I was learning from the Sisters of St. Joseph across the street at St. Mary's, I used to sneak out during study hall and get a bag of donuts or rolls for after school basketball practice. I thought I was quite clever, until one afternoon a famed tough nun, unashamedly called "Ally Oop" by the students —behind her back only, of course— waved a finger at me as I moved down the hall. "Mr. Metivier," she smiled (nuns always smiled when they were scaring you) "I think it would be nice if you brought back a bag of those jelly donuts you are about to get at the Mohican for some of us good sisters who will be working here after school." She became a regular customer, and I never again worried about someone seeing me scoot across Warren Street at 2 p.m.

Jelly donuts, by the way, were for when you were flush with some extra change, maybe you got a buck as the altar boy serving a funeral that morning. When times were tough, it was a dozen snowflake rolls. These delicious, flour-dusted doughy items were usually 19 cents a dozen.

The Mohican was a very special place. It smelled good, everyone in there was customer friendly. What I most remember is that when you purchased several items at the meat counter, the meatman would write down the cost of each on the side of one of the packages and touching the pencil to his lips, figure up the total, which he wrote at the bottom of the column. He never said, "Have a nice day," when he handed you the packages, he always said, "Thank you, come again." And you did!

୬

23

THE NORTHWAY

One of the favorite late Sunday afternoon pastimes growing up in Glens Falls was to sit on the porch at the field house in Crandall Park and see how many cars could get through the traffic light on Glen Street at the Webster Avenue corner on one change of the light.

The lines of traffic coming out of the Adirondacks on a Sunday would be endless. Glens Falls police would shut off the traffic lights in downtown and just let the cars roll through the city. "It was the only way we could get all the traffic through the city on a Sunday night," retired chief Jim Duggan remembers.

Glens Falls police used to be able to control the traffic lights on Glen Street at Monument and Bank Squares from a mounted platform that let them overlook the squares. They would put some of the younger cops in the street, turn off all the lights above and below the squares, and run traffic from these elevated platforms.

"When everything was right we could have two lanes of cars going south at 50 miles an hour," Duggan remembers. The cars would be stopped for the last time at the Webster Avenue light on Glen Street, setting up the game to count southbound cars through each change of the light, then have them pass through the city, go down the hill and into South Glens Falls and south on Route 9 with no interruption.

Traffic was nearly as heavy each Friday as persons leaving New York City and every place in between there and Saratoga, moved north for the weekend. The road was Route 9, and the ride was long. You passed through every community, red lights, local traffic, side streets, stop signs. Going from New York City to Lake George was an eight- to nine-hour ride. No wonder the Delaware & Hudson trains to Lake George were always full.

Some of the problem was solved with the building of the New York State Thruway. Once the super highway was built from Route 17 to Albany, motorists could work their way out of the city and roar through the Catskills to Albany's exit 24 where motorists rejoined Route 9 for the ride north.

Then came the single most important cause for the opening of the entire North Country since Father Isaac Jogues said, "Isn't that a nice lake?" in the late 1600s. Plans for the Adirondack Northway were years in the making. Many wanted it to go west of Saratoga, others wanted it to connect with routes to Vermont. Some objected to having a major interstate go into the Adirondack State Park, saying it violated Article 14 of the Constitution about the forests being kept "forever wild."

In today's environmental climate, the Adirondack Northway, Interstate 87, would never have been built. The necessary permits, the new rules, the number of agencies, commissions, and strident citizens' groups on both sides of the issue would have kept it a dream, not a road.

But in the 1950s and 60s the idea of building roads to everywhere, under the plan of having existing highways in place if they were ever needed by the military to defend the United States, combined with 28-cent-a-gallon gasoline, got miles and miles of concrete ribbon built all over the country.

The Adirondack Northway was to start near Thruway exit 24 and connect finally with Canadian highway 15 at the international border. It would provide car and truck routes from New York City to Montreal, and make travel to the Adirondacks available to millions.

The Northway was not built in one continuous strip, but in sections. The state obtained rights of way through farms, outside villages and towns, and built portions of the road. For several years, the Northway ended at Route 9 in South Glens Falls at what is now exit 17.

A bridge across the Hudson River to the west of Glens Falls had to be built. Its exact site and the route past the city were in controversy for years. A Glens Falls member of the New York

State Senate, insurance executive Nathan Proller, was one of the persons most responsible for getting the Northway completed in the Glens Falls area. There were bitter fights about it going east of Glens Falls, but the engineers and sanity prevailed, and it came up and across the river near the Big Boom, and rolled on toward Lake George along the foothills of the Adirondacks.

The Glens Falls by-pass, as it was labeled by some, was fought bitterly, as merchants said it would empty out the town. "The cars will go right on by, they won't ever stop in Glens Falls," was the cry. It was pointed out that the unending stream of traffic passing through at 50 miles an hour in the present traffic patterns didn't stop either, but the controversy delayed the continuation of the Northway for a few years.

There was an additional controversy as some builders wanted to use blacktop for the road, while others wanted the traditional concrete. The fact that a superior concrete product, Iron Clad, was made here by Glens Falls Cement Company providing local jobs, caused much of the highway to be made out of concrete.

The next big stretch was to be that past Lake George, on the western side of the lake, built up high enough so those driving by would be able to see the lake and the mountains and hopefully get off and visit the area.

The portion of the Northway above Lake George, that going up through the Warrensburg, Chester area, was carefully planned to take full advantage of a natural route, and when it opened was selected by *Parade Magazine*, the Sunday supplement, as, "The Nation's Most Scenic Highway."

Most of the sections were opened when ready, but there were major plans to mark the opening of the road from Lake George north. Instead of cutting a ribbon to mark the opening of the lanes through the Adirondacks, the state had a helicopter fly through the ribbon. Although it nearly crashed trying to catch the ribbon a few feet above the roadway, the opening was quite spectacular, and the Adirondacks were opened to the world.

Several years later, the objections put up by many of the building engineers on the original project were found to have been correct, and a major construction project added a badly needed third lane to the superhighway. Many of the early planners said increases in traffic patterns would cause the need for a third lane and wanted it in the original plans, but arguments that traffic would never increase to that level prevailed. As soon as persons found how easy it was to drive into the North Country, traffic overwhelmed the two lanes through the Glens Falls/ Saratoga area.

I have an especially vivid memory of the building of that portion of the Northway around Saratoga. There was a lot of pressure to bring it up the west side, but interests in the race track wanted the new superhighway to be near Union Avenue to bring fans to and from the historic track each August.

Working in a Saratoga radio station at the time and planning to get married on a Saturday in September, I asked how much time I could have for a honeymoon, a week, perhaps two weeks? "Take as much time as you want," the station manager told me, "we have just sold the transmitting tower site to the state, the Northway will be built through there. Take a year, we are going off the air permanently on Saturday."

⁂

24

HOW THE OLYMPICS WERE SAVED

₰

The 1980 Winter Olympic Games had seemed ill fated. Every Olympics has its problems, but the Lake Placid organizers had far more than a fair share.

One of the leaders in the battle to bring the Winter Games back to the United States, and to the Adirondack village that had hosted the 1932 Winter Games, the village postmaster William MacKenzie, died while judging a preliminary ski jump competition. The other major mover in the plan, the Rev. Bernard Fell, was battling to keep the committee on target, and problems kept popping up everywhere.

The Europeans were against going to this tiny community in the Adirondack Mountains. "You can't hold alpine events without an Alp," said Serge Lange, the organizer of skiing's World Cup and a power in the sport.

Petty differences in the community, people with selfish personal agendas, and some blatant plundering of programs all hurt the LPOC as it moved toward hosting the world in February 1980.

Programs fell behind schedule, contractors complained about being paid in a timely fashion, the press kept pointing out the problems and wondering aloud and in print if Lake Placid could handle this major winter sports undertaking. The pre-Olympics in 1978 and 1979 did some to calm the detractors, but there were enough continuing problems to fuel the fires of discontent.

Enter Petr (cq) Spurney, a professional organizer who was hailed as the savior of the moment. His personality created more problems. Work continued, people were replaced, money was found, and by the time the Games officially opened at the horse show grounds south of the village, the organizers thought most of the major obstacles were behind them.

They had overcome a lack of snow, a lack of money, and endless complaints about bad rooms and overcharging to the press. The *Chicago Sun Times* ran stories showing pictures of the service station with boards placed over the grease pit where their staffers were living. Wire services, foreign reporters, and many American press people beat up on the committee about poor accommodations, overcharging, and lack of organization.

A firebug tried time and time again to burn down the Lake Placid Club, the venerable old resort founded by Godfrey Dewey and home of the many International Olympic Committee members taking advantage of the perks offered by their office to be in Lake Placid for weeks. The Lake Placid Fire Company wound up leaving trucks at the Lake Placid Club, and finally security officers found the former club employee trying to torch the old, wooden structure.

As the long-rehearsed opening ceremonies came to a close, the LPOC breathed a sigh of relief. The athletes had marched out on time, the music had been spectacular, and the hot air balloons had swept across the fields at just the right moment. Let the Games of Winter begin. The ceremonies ended, it was getting cold, a hint of snow, everything was perfect. Except, the buses to pick up the thousands of spectators at the opening ceremonies did not arrive. People stood around, New York State Troopers made frantic calls on their radios. There were no buses. The elaborate transportation system set up to move thousands of people around for the Games—cars were barred from the entire Olympic area except for police and officials—had collapsed.

A Canadian firm had been chosen to provide the necessary transportation. Many had argued against bringing strange drivers and strange equipment into the Lake Placid area during the winter, but the cash-starved organizers leaped at the lowest bid, and besides, Spurney had set it all up, and didn't he know best?

No, the Immigration Service knew best, it had picked up a lot of the drivers for not having work permits in the U.S., and others were lost on the back Adirondack roads. It is estimated that 20,000 persons walked from the opening ceremonies the few miles back into Lake Placid. But, once there, they could not find transportation to return them to their cars, many ten to 13 miles away in parking lots outside the primary Olympic area.

Horror stories of women in high heels walking through a foot of snow, of Troopers carrying half frozen young children, filled the press reports pouring out of Lake Placid. The next day it was worse. Governor Hugh Carey declared a state of emergency, the Games, it seemed, were going to collapse.

Then Carey made a brilliant move. He ordered his no-nonsense Commissioner of Environmental Conservation Robert Flacke of Lake George to take charge of transportation. Some Olympic Committee people resisted, very briefly. Flacke moved in, found the communications system for transportation nearly non-existent and the few Canadian bus drivers left lost and having no way to get around an area they knew nothing about.

Thousands of spectators, the press, the athletes, and officials had to be moved, every day. The alpine ski events were 13 miles away at Whiteface Mountain. The sliding and cross country skiing events were seven to 10 miles out of town, and spectators were miles from their cars.

Could things get worse? Sure. President Jimmy Carter announced a boycott of the Summer Olympic Games because of disputes with Russia, and things got ugly.

Flacke, who had brought Encon into the second half of the 20th century with new management policies and programs quickly took over, evaluated the transportation nightmare, and made a vital decision.

A close aide of Governor Carey's, the Lake George businessman commissioner had been among those sent by the worried state earlier to sort out some of the organizational problems at Lake Placid. He had helped Rev. Fell and others to get things back on track, got some needed cash and in-kind help from the state, assistance from the federales, and calmed down the Europeans, but now Flacke faced his biggest challenge ever.

His overnight decision saw him press the Encon radio system into use, giving the transportation unit some decent communication facilities. Then he ordered all the area school buses to take over the transportation system.

Schools throughout the Lake Placid region were closed for the duration of the Games, and the buses were garaged. Flacke told the veteran school bus drivers to use their experience to find routes when main roads were clogged with people, and to leave when the bus was full, not when a number written on a piece of paper said to go.

He established a transportation system for the athletes, the press, officials, and most importantly the people holding tickets who were parked miles from the venue where they wanted to see an event.

It worked. The bus drivers were used to the snow and ice of the roads, they all knew back routes to everywhere, and soon transportation was not a problem for the 1980 Winter Games.

Flacke's reward for his rescue of the 1980 Winter Games was that when he backed New York Mayor Ed Koch in the primary campaign for governor, and Mario Cuomo won, Flacke was back in Lake George running his business, and a Cuomo supporter became Encon commissioner.

ε&

25

SOUNDS OF MUSIC

In organizing its annual budget during 1992, the City of Glens Falls had one of the same problems facing all levels of government, lack of money. Faced with laying off employees and cutting essential programs, the city fathers had to also do away with several long-term activities the funding of which could no longer be justified.

Among these were the Thursday evening concerts by the Glens Falls City Band on the bandstand in City Park. "We could not justify terminating employees and still fund the band concerts," the mayor stated, pointing out no one wanted to end the music shows but fairness and common sense —which still is part of small town government in many cases— called for the elimination of the summer music programs.

No one paid much attention during the snow months, there was plenty in the budget cuts to keep everyone's attention and the elimination of the band concerts went nearly unnoticed. Then came June and news the Thursday night programs would not be held during the summer of 1992.

The usual anger, outrage and railing against government never took place since the reasons the city had used to eliminate funding the programs made sense. While lots of people enjoyed the music, it could not be funded while veteran employees were laid off due to a lack of cash.

The city's alternative newspaper, the weekly *Chronicle*, which has always had a good sense of its community, started calling around to some of its long time advertisers. A downtown business group did the same. Sandy's Clam Bar, a long-time tough spot on South Street, which has now become a yuppie watering hole, immediately came through with a $2,000 donation. Others, including the Musician's Performance Fund, matched it, and the band concerts were fully funded for the summer season without the city ponying up cent one.

What is this Thursday night summer ritual in flower-filled City Park that brought out such response from a populace usually concerned about spending fewer taxpayer dollars on programs, not for picking up the funding once it is cut by government?

During the early part of the 1940s, after the local National Guard unit had been mobilized and shipped out prior to the beginning of World War II, the State Guard stepped in and took over. Part of the State Guard unit was the Second Regiment Band. It was made up of many young high school musicians and older players not eligible for active duty with the Guard.

"We were members of the State Guard, we got shots and uniforms, and in the summer we got to go to Camp Smith in Peekskill," remembers trumpet player Robert "Red" LaFera. At 15, LaFera and several of his Glens Falls High School band companions found themselves in a military band, playing concerts in the park and march music for parades. "It was great for us young guys," LaFera remembered, "we got to play in a real band with older musicians, we learned a lot about music. There were a few very good players, one who had played with the Sousa Band in Washington."

The Second Regiment Band provided music through the end of the War, and when LaFera returned home from service in the U.S. Navy at the very end of the war, he found the Glens Falls City Band had been formed from the remnants of the Second Regiment Band.

"We started playing band concerts in the park again, played in parades, it was pretty informal, just music people wanted to hear," LaFera said. "The park would be full for the concerts. We used to take a break in the middle and on warm nights the guys would go over to the Wonder Bar on Maple Street during the intermission. We started getting paid, but the most I ever earned for a band concert was $6."

Band concerts were a part of growing up in Glens Falls. The stores stayed open on Thursdays, everyone went downtown, got a bag of popcorn from the Five and Dime and ended up strolling around the park, listening to music and trying to find someone to walk home. It was the coming of age in Hometown U.S.A., part of the rites of passage.

Young marrieds would return with their first borns in a carriage and tool around the same sidewalks where they had first held hands in high school, listening to the music. Old folks would sit on the worn green benches, kids would play, teen-agers would toss Frisbies, and the cops lucky enough to have gotten the beat would walk the perimeter, tipping their caps in greeting to the old ladies they helped across Ridge Street and twirling their nightsticks on the end of a long rawhide thong.

Band concerts in Glens Falls City Park could have been designed by Norman Rockwell. No other event cried out, "This **IS** Hometown, U.S.A." as much as two hours of music from the bandstand.

The bandstand is its own story. There was one in the center of the park for decades. Open on all sides, with a four-sided roof, it was where the politicians spoke on holidays, prizes were given out for the city party on Halloween, bright young high school students presented Lincoln's immortal words on Memorial Day, and Santa ho-hoed when he arrived by firetruck each Friday after Thanksgiving.

One of the biggest crowds ever seen at the bandstand was the late night when Bobby Kennedy arrived at 2 a.m., campaigning for Congress. He and his amazed aides looked out onto the sea of Glens Falls faces, of people holding their kids in pajamas. Kennedy told the group he was sorry to be so late, could not believe everyone had hung around for hours, and that the day after election—win or lose—he would be back. True to his word, Kennedy came back the day after his victory; 10,000 people filled the park, and every politician within 50 miles tried to get on the groaning bandstand.

When it was decided, in the 1970s, that the old bandstand needed major repairs, word spread that a new, modern music shell might be built. City Hall got the word, quickly, and plans were drawn to reproduce the bandstand. The new one was four sided, white, and had a shingle roof, just no dry rot in the wood, and a built-in sound system to make it different from the old bandstand.

A dedication concert by the Glens Falls City Band drew scores of people who wanted to remember their happy days of listening to music and trying to get a date to visit a pharmacy for a coke and a walk home. The new bandstand passed inspection, and City Hall breathed a sign of relief, another bullet dodged. One Council member got up during a meeting and waved a fistfull of bills, decrying the amount of money spent on building the new bandstand. The mayor and the other council people just smiled. There are places to spend money, and there are great places to spend money. The new bandstand was a win/win project.

The new bandstand became even more a part of life in the city. Each Christmas, fresh-cut trees were put inside the stand, decorated and lighted. The sound system is used to pipe holiday music out into the park. More flowers, extra trees, new donated lights cast soft shadows on the sidewalks. City Park gives the city a heart, a gathering place. Each June, a massive craft show has 200 booths fill the park, and entertainment continues non-stop from the Bandstand.

Each Tuesday evening during the summer, the Glens Falls Band plays a band concert in the old bandstand in Warrensburg, and each Wednesday the musicians move to the new village music shell on the shores of Lake George. But Thursdays are for tradition. The sound of march music and big band tunes wafts across City Park, up into the Cronin high-rise apartments for the elderly, across the sidewalks where teenagers walk holding hands, and young couples push their babies, and into the windows of those guests of the Queensbury Hotel lucky enough to have their rooms facing Maple Street.

A great story from the Queensbury is when a desk clerk received a call from a guest who complained, he was a regular at the hotel and had always had a room facing the park on Thursdays. A new clerk had put him on the other side of the hotel. They found an empty room over Maple Street and moved him just in time for the overture.

ᏽ

26

A SPECIAL HORSE

ॐ

It was a morning like most in late July in a very special place called Saratoga. The main track was filled with sweating, snorting, frisky, full-of-themselves thoroughbreds trying to get in shape for the season that was to begin in a few days.

There was a special three year old out on the soft, comfortable Saratoga race strip, a nice-looking colt from Meadow Stable called Riva Ridge. This was no ordinary colt, but a runner Penny Tweedy had given to trainer Lucien Lauren to bring through a tremendous two-year-old campaign that saw him win seven of nine starts and more than a half million dollars in purses. As a three year old, Riva Ridge had won the Kentucky Derby, which is enough to gain instant immortality in this sport of paupers and kings. He missed in the Preakness, but came back to win the 1972 Belmont Stakes, two events of the Triple Crown, and had come to Saratoga to prep for the Travers, the famed Midsummer Derby.

Groom Eddie Sweat led him out for an early morning work out, and exercise rider George Davis was relaxed in the irons, enjoying the attention given to a great horse and its rider.

Riva Ridge had not come through the Triple Crown in the best of shape, and his work was good, but not what Lauren wanted. Davis guided the nice colt back through the trees toward Barn 19 and Sweat dropped back, carrying his pail and a lead halter. "You goin' to breakfast now?" he asked. Assured I was, he smiled and said, "I got to rub and walk this colt, but after you eat come by the barn, I got somethin' special for you to see."

Grooms tout their horses more than trainers, much more than owners, and all want to have one great runner. Eddie Sweat had groom's trophies from the Kentucky Derby and the Belmont, more than most who toil in the barns ever get for a career in the backstretch.

The horsemen's kitchen was filled with its regulars, trainers, assistant trainers, agents looking to hustle rides for their jockeys, some long-time owners who enjoyed sitting at the faded picnic tables covered with an oilcloth in the kitchen, rather than with the fresh cut flowers on a table in the clubhouse. When you eat in the Backstretch Kitchen on a semi-regular basis, you don't order, you take the eggs cooked the way you like them, the fresh cut slices of Virginia ham, the fried potatoes, toast, and strong coffee in a quarter-pound mug they hand you, since they know that's your regular morning meal, and tradition is strong in the backstretch.

Breakfast over, time to walk to the barn. Eddie Sweat is just putting Riva Ridge away, the sudsy bath finished, the rubdown complete, and the hot walk over. "Just in time, just in time," he smiles, unhooks the lead halter from "the Ridge" and puts him into the stall just filled with fresh straw. The stable dog barks a welcome, and a couple of late hangers-on from the New York press corps nod hello.

"Hey, you're a skier," one of them says, "isn't this colt named for some ski trail out west?"

"Almost," I tell him. "Penny Tweedy has a home at Vail in Colorado, and Vail was organized by a guy named Pete Seibert. Seibert was a member of the 10th Mountain Division in the War, the ski troops. The ski troops beat up the Germans in a big battle in Italy, it helped the good guys to get through the mountains and up into Germany. It was a major battle of the war, the biggest for the 10th Mountain guys. It was fought at a place called Riva Ridge. So when Seibert comes home and builds Vail, he names one of the runs Riva Ridge to honor the 10th Mountain guys who fought in the battle.

"When Tweedy gets this nice colt, she asks Seibert if she can name it Riva Ridge too, and he says sure."

The city writer has been making copious notes, "Thanks, thanks a lot," he says, hurrying away to write his column.

"Why do you tell him all that good shit?" Sweat says to me, "he'll write that like he knows all about that war stuff himself." I shrug, and Sweat and I smile together because he knows why

I told the story, now extra millions will know about the ski troopers.

"Get over here, my man," Sweat says. We go over to a stall, he takes a lead chain from a hook on the side of the old green wooden barn, snaps it into the ring on a halter and brings out a massive colt.

"This here," the old groom says, "is the bestest race horse in the history of the world. He's only two, he is gonna go in the Sanford, and he can run faster than any colt in the history of the world."

So, at about 8 a.m. on Wednesday, July 26, 1972, I met a colt named Secretariat. "He's just a baby," Sweat said, "he ain't done nothin' yet, but he's big, he's fast, and he's got heart."

Secretariat was impressive in the morning light. Big, high of shoulder, obviously strong, and if this old man said he could run, then he probably could. Lauren walked by. "Lookin' at my new star?" the French-born trainer asked. "Write that name down, this guy is going to be a champion."

The Sanford has been a test for two year olds at Saratoga since its first running in 1913. The most familiar legend about the stakes is the defeat of Man o' War by Upset in the Sanford of 1919. As it turned out, it was the only loss on an otherwise unbeaten record. Off to a bad start, Man o' War made up all but half a length. In later years, Willie Knapp, rider of Upset would say, "I've always been kind of sorry I beat him. He was too much of a horse for that."

Lauren sent Secretariat out in the Sanford with rider Ron Turcotte in the irons. The colt eased home in front, covering the six furlongs in 1:10 flat. No horse had ever done that before, and none would do it again until Affirmed won the 1977 event in 1:09 3/5 prior to going on to his Triple Crown championship season.

"Nothin, nothin'," Sweat said back at the barn cooling the big colt down. "Wait until the Hopeful, he's ready."

The Hopeful, at 6 1/2 furlongs, is the biggest test for two year olds. It is the first time they have ever run that far, and it attracts the best youngsters in the country. The list of winners is filled with colts now in the Racing Hall of Fame just across Union Avenue from the track: Regret, Man o' War, Whirlaway, Native Dancer, Nashua, and Buckpasser are just a few of the Hopeful champions. Its name means that owners who drop entries into the field are hopeful that they have colts of classic possibilities.

Mrs. Tweedy and Lauren couldn't wait to enter Secretariat. Turcotte brought the big colt through the pack to get the win in the 68th running on the fourth Saturday in August, 1972, and Meadow Stable had a new star. It helped to overcome the disappointment of not even getting Riva Ridge to the post in the Travers.

"What I tell you, what I tell you," Sweat chanted back at the barn. "When we come back up here next summer, when I see you again in this backstretch, me and this big guy will have won the Triple Crown."

And the rest, as they say, is history!

❧

27

THE SUMMER
OF SECRETARIAT

&

When Secretariat came back to New York after winning the Kentucky Derby and the Preakness in 1973, everyone expected him to win the Belmont Stakes.

No one expected him to destroy the field, winning by more than 20 lengths in the track and a Stakes record time of 2:24 for the mile and a half, in what most veteran observers of the horse racing game believe was the most dominating victory in the history of the Triple Crown.

How dominating was the Belmont Stakes win? Harbor View Farms' Triple Crown winner Affirmed won the 1978 Belmont over a strong field in 2:26 4/5, and Loblolly Stables' fine colt Temperence (cq) Hill won in 1980 in 2:29 4/5. That is nearly six seconds slower than Secretariat.

So when Meadow Stables trailered Secretariat to Saratoga, the entire 1973 meeting was to revolve around the big colt. Trainer Lucien (cq) Lauren had to meet a huge press corps on a regular basis. Jockey Ron Turcotte was one of the most sought-after interviews in the Spa city, and photographers were given carefully arranged "photo opportunities" to shoot pictures of the Triple Crown winner, so he would not be disturbed in his training program.

The colt was on the track early each morning for his workouts, and soon morning crowds were exceeding 5,000. People lined the rail each day at dawn. Parents held their children up to see Secretariat go by. The horse was one of sports' great heroes, bigger than life, a legend.

Back in the barn all was not going as well as the Secretariat connections would like. The excitement, the tremendous strain of the Triple Crown events, three races in five weeks in the spring over ever increasing distances, all this had taken its toll on the champion. Eddie Sweat, his groom, was worried. "He has given so much, he needs some rest," he said about his most famous charge.

Lauren would sit high in the stands under the roof of the club house in the mornings, keeping out of view of the hordes of press, and watch the works, usually with Secretariat's regular rider Ron Turcotte up.

"He's tired, but he's got so much heart," Lauren said one dawn as we gulped coffee I had brought down from the press hutch on the roof. "He only knows one way to run, all out."

There was tremendous pressure on the Secretariat group to get the great horse onto the track. Usually colts prep for the running of the Midsummer Derby, the Travers Stakes, by running in the mile-and-an-eighth Jim Dandy. The race was named for the horse that had posted one of the great upsets of all time at Saratoga, beating the immortal Gallant Fox in the 1930 Travers. Jim Dandy had won that Travers at odds of 100 to one.

Saratoga was still holding its four-week season in 1973, and the first Saturday feature would be the Whitney Handicap for three year olds and up. For a variety of reasons, most of it reaction to pressure from the racing fraternity, Secretariat was entered in the mile-and-an-eighth Whitney, an event that usually attracts older horses.

Saratoga's favorite horse, before Secretariat, had been the champion Kelso. Banners with his name were stretched across Broadway in Downtown Saratoga and there was even a "Kelso Day" in the Spa city. Kelso won the 1961 Whitney as a four year old, came back to win in 1963, and then as an eight year old, won the 1965 Whitney lugging 130 pounds.

Now Secretariat was to be asked to run with older horses in his prep for the Travers. It had worked the year before as Rokeby Stable had run Key to the Mint in the Whitney as a prep. He won the Jim Dandy and came back to win the 1972 Travers as well.

News that Secretariat was to run in the Whitney brought out more morning railbirds to watch the colt get ready to challenge the older horses on Saturday. A huge crowd was on hand for the race, and the Meadow Stable colt went off as an odds-on favorite.

Turcotte kept him on the pace, but in the stretch an unknown four year old with the unlikely name "Onion" pulled away to win in the very ordinary time of 1:49 1/5 giving Hobeau Farm the victory and sending thousands home disappointed.

Secretariat came out of the Whitney not only defeated, but an even more tired horse. He continued to work before big crowds as the Saratoga season wore on, but it was obvious he was not in the same form that had seen him demolish the field in the Belmont.

During Travers week Lauren made an announcement that Secretariat would not run in the race on Saturday. That kept Whirlaway's record intact as the only Triple Crown winner in history to come on and win the Travers. Sir Barton, Omaha, War Admiral, Count Fleet, Assault, and Citation, previous Triple Crown champions, had also not been able to answer the call to the post for the Travers, and Gallant Fox had been upset at the wire by Jim Dandy as was the only other Triple Crown winner to challenge a Travers' field.

On Saturday, before the horses took to the track for the 104th running of America's oldest event for three year olds, Secretariat took a turn around the track with Turcotte up. The big colt perked his ears as he started down the long Saratoga stretch at a lope. He heard the noise of the crowd start to swell and the big colt responded by moving faster than Turcotte had planned. As he came past the grandstand and then the club house, the cheers rocked the old wooden stands as thousands stood in tribute to one of the greatest race horses in history.

Lauren brought Secretariat back into shape and got him ready for the first running of the rich Marlboro Cup Invitational Handicap at Belmont Park in early September. Turcotte took him out quickly, and he ran away to win in 1:45 2/5, nearly four seconds faster than Onion's time in the Whitney. Secretariat carried 124 pounds in the Marlboro, Onion had won the Whitney with 119 pounds.

The enormous amount of money offered to take him off the track and put him in the stud barn won out over pleas to let him run as a four year old. A massive syndicate was organized, and Secretariat went into stud for more money than any horse in previous racing history. With Secretariat out of the picture, Forego, from the Lazy F Ranch, who had not figured in the three-year-old events, came on to be the best of the older horses, dominating the handicap events for several seasons.

During the Saratoga meeting of the summer of 1974, Secretariat became the horse most quickly elected to the Racing Hall of Fame. All of his connections were on hand as the Triple Crown winner was enshrined in the Racing Museum's Hall of Fame on Union Avenue just across from the track.

Lauren, who had trained back-to-back Kentucky Derby winners and brought Secretariat to superstar status (and was himself to be elected to the Hall of Fame in 1977) was on hand.

"How's it going?" I asked, as we stood in the back and listened to the speeches touting his most famous charge. "OK," he smiled, "but I sure would like to be across the street with him as a four year old. He's just maturing. We will never know just how good he could have been."

They should have left him on the track, because that was where his talent shined. As a stud, he turned out to be anything but a superstar. Eddie Sweat said it best: "He left it all on the track."

ॐ

28

YADDO

ੋੰ

"Build it, and they will come," they were told in the motion picture "Field of Dreams." At Yaddo, that story has been reality for more than 65 years.

Yaddo was the dream of Spencer and Katrina Trask, the dream of turning their Saratoga Springs estate into a retreat for writers, poets, composers, sculptors, and thinkers.

It was not an Iowa cornfield, but a Saratoga pine forest in 1899 where Katrina told her husband: "Here will be a perpetual series of house parties —of literary men, literary women, and other artists. Those who are city weary, who are thirsting for the country and for beauty, who are hemmed in by circumstances. Look, Spencer, they are walking in the woods, wandering in the garden, sitting under the pine trees —men and women—creating, creating, creating."

Since 1926 they have come, and their creations have made literary, musical, and creative history. Set up as a trust, the Corporation of Pine Garde has provided a place for creating for hundreds of men and women. The famous, Saul Bellow, Susan Cheever, Philip Roth, Truman Capote, Eudora Welty, painter Milton Avery, and composers Aaron Copland and Ned Rorem, and scores more whose work fill the libraries, museums, and musical repertory of the world, as well as others who have made their contributions to the overall quality of life the arts provides, have created at Yaddo.

The Trasks came to Saratoga in 1881, and scorned purchasing one of the "cottages" on North Broadway, but instead took over the Child property along Union Avenue near the famed Saratoga Racecourse.

Mrs. Trask wrote, "It is much more clever and interesting to make a locality fashionable than it is to take a fashionable locality." So much for North Broadway.

The original house on the property burned in 1881, and the present 55-room Yaddo mansion was built on the foundations of the first by Spencer Trask in 1893.

Yaddo was named by the Trask's daughter, Christina, who said it sounded like "shadow," but the popular story about the name, is that it was called Yaddo by the Trask son who liked to see his shadow in the pool, where he later drowned. No part of that tale is true.

The Trask family was struck repeatedly by tragedy. The family had come to Saratoga to help overcome the grief from the death of their son Alan. Christina died in April 1888 at 11, and Junius died three days later. The children were thought to have contacted diphtheria from Katrina, who recovered from the disease. In 1889, their last child died 12 days after birth, and Yaddo became the focal point of their lives.

Using the pine and rose emblems of Spencer and Katrina, they developed Yaddo and its grounds. A combination of castle and cottage, it was a gathering place for the famous of the day. They collected furniture and built the huge mansion into a hospitable building.

Much of the furniture has been in place since the 19th century, giving the building a sense of stability, and giving the hundreds of creative persons who have labored there on projects a sense of well being. Many have written and spoken about being able to work better within the comforting confines of Yaddo than in any other place.

Spencer was killed in a train crash in 1909, and Katrina became almost a recluse. She moved out of the mansion and into a converted caretaker's cottage in 1916, to save funds for the Yaddo project she saw so clearly. However, she would not allow it to begin until after her death.

In 1920, she married her husband's long-time business part- ner George Foster Peabody. He pressured her to hire a director and to let the Yaddo project begin. Katrina told Peabody she would not name a director: "She will come when it is time for her to come," she told her new husband shortly before she died in 1921.

When Mrs. Elizabeth Ames came to visit her sister, who was working at Yaddo with Peabody on a research project, Peabody knew the director had arrived. Mrs. Ames remained as the Yaddo director and leader through 1970, forever shaping the rules, the tone, the spirit, and programs that have made it one of the most successful artist retreats in the world.

There are as many great stories of Yaddo itself as there are stories that have been written there. Nellie Shannon, who was chased from her home and work in her native Newfoundland by the War, was hired by Mrs. Ames as the cook in 1946 and was there 40 years. She became a confidant to writers, composers, and poets, often sitting in the kitchen late at night to discuss a work in progress. Her chief legacy, in addition to some great literary works she helped develop, was her bread pudding recipe, which is still carefully followed by some of the finest creative minds in America. Nellie married James Shannon in 1951, a worker at Yaddo as well, having been Peabody's driver for many years.

To help his wife overcome her grief following the death of the children, Spencer Trask worked at developing gardens and streams on the Yaddo grounds. He laid out the rose gardens in 1899 and dedicated them to Katrina.

Katrina was truly the "queen" of the manor, and the family made that official on Halloween in 1882. They wrote and carried out a private but elaborate ceremony that named Kate Nichols Trask, "Katrina, Queen of Yaddo," and presented her with a crown, ring, sword, and scepter. Following the coronation, she always used her royal name, Katrina.

While Yaddo has been providing rooms, meals, a place to create and think to "guests" for nearly 70 years, the funds left in trust for the sanctuary have recently not provided enough to cover the costs of keeping up the house and its programs. An ongoing series of fund raisers have been held, and thanks to scores of dedicated volunteers, money has always been available to continue the plan Katrina saw in her view of the future almost a century ago.

Her will ordered that while the guests working in the mansion and the out buildings were not to be disturbed, the gardens were to be open to the public, "from 8 a.m. to dusk," every day.

Hundreds of thousands of visitors have toured the gardens and marveled at the roses. Hundreds of couples have been married in ceremonies held in the gardens. For decades, couples have returned to show their children the place where many proposed, and others were married.

The cost of keeping up the house and the hosting of the guests in a creative atmosphere finally took its toll on the grounds. The gardens were kept, but the rose garden was not what it was years ago. But Katrina's plan that "she will come when it is time for her to come" worked again. Jane Wait, who had long been involved with Yaddo and many other Saratoga civic programs, working with other volunteers, organized the Yaddo Garden Association in late 1991. By mid-1992, membership topped 60 and was growing, as were new roses. A special Rose Remembrance program had persons donate $10 to plant a rose bush in the gardens in memory of a loved one. Response to the new plan was enormous, and hundreds of new roses were planted in the gardens now lovingly tended by an ever-increasing number of volunteers.

The miracle of Yaddo continues. The stability, the source of artistic inspiration, "Yaddo Life" as seen by the Trasks, is alive and well. They built it, and they came, "creating, creating, creating."

☙

29

FATHER LEDUC

ૐ

Growing up in Glens Falls, you learned the ground rules about many things early. One of the first things you learned was that St. Mary's was the Irish church, and St. Alphonsus was the French church.

There had been no Vatican II, you couldn't join the YMCA and go to St. Mary's Academy, Glens Falls Insurance Company did not hire young women who had just graduated from St. Mary's, and at the Glens Falls Post Company, a young woman's diploma should note graduation from the Academy, not the high school.

We lived with these things, not even knowing the implications of what they meant. While there might have been out and out discrimination by the adult populace, the kids paid no attention. One of the town's fine athletes was Dewey Sims. He used to say he didn't know he was black until he got to Xavier to play football. "No one ever mentioned it," he used to say, "but they made up for it in New Orleans when I was going to college."

I learned early about the two churches. My mother was Irish, my father French, although he had a Dwyer for a mother, so only his name and half his ancestry were French.

The pastor at St. Mary's was an intellectual Irishman named Rt. Rev. Msgr. Joseph P. Kelly. He wrote books, including the history of the parish, and gave sermons where everyone nodded in agreement, but didn't really understand. He was fluent in several languages, had influential friends, drove a big car, and sort of floated about two feet over the head of Joe Sixpack and his kids from the East End, the Irish and the Italians who filled St. Mary's.

The pastor at St. Alphonsus was a tough former boxer, Navy guy, a two-fisted, plain-talking French priest, who also got the Bishop to name him a monsignor, the Rt. Rev. Msgr. Paul Leduc. When Paul Leduc gave a sermon, you never had to ask anyone what he meant. He said what he meant in short, punchy sentences.

One Sunday, right after Memorial Day, the altar rail —they still had altar rails then—was covered with tin cans, old bottles, broken drinking glasses and other assorted trash.

Right after the gospel—you remember the gospel, now it's the third reading—Father Leduc came to the front of the altar where he always stood to give his sermons. Some of the priests walked up into the pulpit alongside the altar, but he didn't need a pulpit or a microphone.

"You see this garbage here," he said, pointing to the stuff on the altar rail. "I picked this stuff up in our cemetery. We don't put flowers in beer bottles in our cemetery, we don't put plants in tin cans, and the dead don't appreciate you being slobs in their home."

For the next few minutes, he outlined his rules for putting flowers in St. Alphonsus Cemetery. After mass, my grand-pere and some of his cronies piled into the truck he used to deliver orders from the market to his customers and they went to the cemetery. They picked the place up, tossed all the junk into the truck, and left it at the dump on the way to get a snort or two and talk over their good deed for the week.

Needless to say, not a lot of people ever put flowers in a beer bottle and left it on a grave again.

The French nuns who labored in the vineyard that was St. Alphonsus School—a fire-trap wooden structure next to the big church, the church burned but they had to tear the old school down— reported they were having problems with some of the little ones in kindergarten. It seems they were not fully potty trained.

Enter Msgr. Leduc at the children's mass, which is universally 9 a.m. everywhere in the Catholic world. One of the other priests was saying mass, but the pastor showed up to preach. He told of how the "good sisters" had studied at their convent in

Canada, learning to bring a good Catholic education and the teachings of the church to the "little ones in their charge." He said how important it was that the children spent those years learning self-discipline and arithmetic as well as the capital of Idaho. He pointed out that the sisters were "full of sacrifice," and would use all their strength to bring the fear of God and grammar to the children of this parish.

"However," he bellowed, his giant, ham-sized hand sweeping in an arc that would make an NBA center proud, "these good women are not here to potty train your babies. Before you send your angels to St. Alphonsus, we not only think you should teach them to drink, but to undrink as well."

No one peed in his pants again in kindergarten, not ever.

One of the celebrations held only at St. Alphonsus was a mass at 4 a.m. on New Year's Day. There was midnight mass at Christmas everywhere. A lot of my Protestant friends would ask to go with me and my folks to midnight mass at St. Mary's. The choir would sing Christmas hymns, the organ would pour out the glorious news that Christ was born in Bethlehem, and the priests would be resplendent in their gold robes. The sweet smell of incense would fill the big church as the tallest of the altar boys got to swing the sensor and make the smoke "rise to heaven." It was a great show.

One year, a Jewish kid up the street asked if he could go. My mother thought it might be a sacrilege, but my dad, who was light years ahead of his time, said, "You can go. Just watch us, do what we do." The kid stood up, knelt down, sat down, sang, and folded his hands right on cue. But when we left the pew to go up to communion, that was too much for my mother. "You sit down, no kneel down, and wait here." She wasn't sure if we should go to communion ourselves since bringing him might have been a serious sin, or at least a venial sin. Remember venial sins?

But the 4 a.m. mass at St. Alphonsus was unique to that church and obviously a marketing success. The crowds that would be out celebrating New Year's Eve would be ready to go home about 3:30, and the idea of dropping by St. Alphonsus for a mass at 4 and not having to get up again until the bowl games came on the radio was appealing. It was go to the 4 on the way home, or get up and go to the 12. That was no decision, the 4 was always packed.

No one talked much about going to the 4 a.m. mass, probably because no one remembered much of what happened. Father Leduc always said that mass himself. I remember the first time I was allowed to go. The family had celebrated New Year's Eve at Billy Angleson's Esquire, a fancy joint on South Street where my Uncle Ken Usher and Joe Lawlor tended bar. The Esquire had one of the first television sets ever in a Glens Falls bar. My dad and I used to go there every Tuesday at 8 to watch Milton Berle on the Texaco program. We would have a Number 5, which was a glorified club sandwich. I got a Coke, and my dad always had Saratoga vichy. He never drank when he was younger.

So, on New Year's I was allowed to go along with aunts, uncles, a cousin or two, parents, and my Irish grandmother, who always took her Canadian Club in milk. Right after midnight I was dispatched down the street to my grandmother's in the Savoy Apartments, where I could listen to the big bands on the radio, as New Year's came in across the country.

About 3:45 my folks picked me up, and I teased to go to the 4 a.m. mass. As usual, my mother was horrified, my father thought it was a great idea.

The place was full. The pews were stuffed, and the place smelled like one of the old gin mills my grand pere used to make quick stops in when we were delivering groceries.

There was no sermon. What do you say to a church filled with sleeping celebrants. Father Leduc saved his comments for the offertory.

"Most of the people in here are tired. They have been welcoming in the new year of our Lord 1949. We do not want to disturb these good people, so I would ask there be no unnecessary noise during the collection. We provide this early morning mass and we ask that you provide a New Year's offering for God's church. You had enough money to celebrate, now put some of that quiet money into the basket. God bless you. Happy New Year."

There was the soft rustle of bills being dropped into the basket as the sleepy usher moved down the aisle. I reached into my pocket and horror filled my brain. "I've only got a quarter," I said much too loudly to my father.

"Here," the sleeping drunk on the other side of me said, handing me a dollar. "Put this in for me," he said before going back to sleep.

Vignette 1. Broadway looking south from Post Office, 1958, Saratoga, NY.

Vignette 1. Grand Union Hotel, Saratoga, NY.

Historical Society of Saratoga Springs.

Historical Society of Saratoga Springs.

❧ **Vignette 1.** Laraine and Don Metivier dancing at the Saratoga Perfoming Arts Center Gala Ball, Hall of Springs.

≈ *Vignette 2. The Sagamore Hotel in the early days, about 1900.*

≈ *Vignette 2. The Sagamore Hotel in the 1940s.*

ક **Vignette 5.**
*Calvin Coolidge's autographed
picture to Doc Cook.*

ક **Vignette 7.**
*Walk to the
paddock on race
day at Saratoga.*

ક **Vignette 8.**
*The Halfway
House—known
from Coast to
Coast.*

  Vignette 10.
Brownell sisters
admire the annual
bloom on their
cereus plant.

  Vignette 11.
Charles Evans Hughes,
namesake of the Hughes Ban.

  Vignette 14.
Sammy Davis, Jr. and Jerry Lewis.

🌱 *Vignette 20. Harry D. Elkes' grave.*

Vignette 24. Area around Lake Placid— site of 1980 Winter Olympics.

Vignette 25. Glens Falls City Band 1950s.

Frederic Chase.

Vignette 25. Glens Falls bandstand at Christmas.

ka *Vignette 26.*
Eddie Sweat, groom,
with his charge,
Secretariat, 1973.

ka *Vignette 27.*
Secretariat's trainer,
Lucien Lauren, under
Clubhouse roof,
August 1973.

ka *Vignette 28.*
Yaddo Estate,
Saratoga Springs,
NY.

ॐ *Vignette 29.*
Rt. Rev. Msgr.
Paul A. Leduc.

ॐ *Vignette 30.*
Maestro Eugene
Ormandy with
Philadelphia
Orchestra at
Saratoga Perform-
ing Arts Center.

ॐ *Vignette 34.*
André Watts is
one of
Saratoga's
favorite
musicians.

❦ *Vignette 35. H. C. Metivier's Market, South Street.*

❦ *Vignette 35. Anthony H. Metivier (father) and Henry C. Metivier (grandfather) on the porch of H.C. Metivier's Market on Lincoln Ave. in Glens Falls.*

🔊 *Vignette 36. Downtown Glens Falls, NY, in photo taken for* Look *magazine, 1943.*

🔊 *Vignette 36.*
Jerry Grennon watches Cosmo Palange sharpen scissors. Photo taken for Look *magazine.*

Vignette 37. They're off at Saratoga!

Vignette 39. Don Metivier with General William Westmoreland.

Vignette 40.
Muffin, the junk food dog.

Vignette 42.
Metiviers' Christmas tree.

Vignette 43.
Stella Taylor
swimming the
32-mile length
of Lake George.

❧ *Vignette 44. Lake George.*

❧ *Vignette 48.*
The New Way
Lunch, one of the
last great hot dog
emporiums.

❧ Vignette 50. Blue Moutain Lake during the fall.

❧ Rockwell Falls, Lake Lucerne, NY.

❧ *Hudson River above Glens Falls.*

❧ *Trout Pavilion on Lake George.*

❧ *Rip Van Dam Hotel Saratoga Springs, NY.*

When the basket got in front of me, I grinned at the usher and dropped in the bill, not making a sound. I was very grown up that year.

ᏃᏆ

30

PLAYING THE NUMBERS

ॠ

There is a major trend these days among the older people having babies, to give their little miracles early exposure to the good things in life. You see them with the tykes at symphony concerts. Take a six month old to the Philadelphia Orchestra, and it will grow up to love good music and quite possibly be another Eugene Ormandy. At least that's the theory.

The fact the poor baby is tired, could care less about the music, and annoys everyone around them doesn't phase these people. The father grins, and the mother looks proud.

Well, I was brought up with a hands-on plan in place as well. When I was about six or seven, my grand pere taught me to drag the old wooden milk box out of the back room at the market, where the insurance lady used it to stand on to reach the coin box on the slot machine, to put it near the phone so I could reach to make a call.

Grand pere had the two numbers I could call about 2:30 each afternoon written on the wall. In fact, there were a couple of hundred numbers on the wall: Swift and Co. for chickens; Armour for beef; First Prize for cold meat; the name of the farmers where he bought veggies; Adirondack Dairy and Jiglies for milk and cream; Hovey's for fruit; Ray's Beverage for soda; WGY Grocery for canned goods; NBC Bread; Dane-T-Bits for cookies; the Italian store on Lawrence Street for sausage; and Derby's Bakery for jelly donuts, lots of important numbers.

My grandmother had her own list of numbers up there too, but off by themselves. She had the number of the card room next door, of Clover Joubert's tap room down the street, of the horseroom over Rocky's and Brownie's pool room. She kept those numbers handy in case she needed my grand-pere in a hurry to grind a few pounds of hamburg or cut a crown roast. Usually if he was next door in the card room she didn't waste a phone call, but just beat on the wall with a broom handle, and he would hurry back to the meat market.

But each afternoon I was to get the milk bottle box, drag it out of the tiny little slot machine room, put it near the phone mounted on the wall near the slicing machine, and call for the "first two."

You must remember that in those wonderful times, the State of New York did not run the horserooms —now they do, and call it OTB— or the numbers, which is now known as the New York State Lottery. Bookies like Red, Harry the Horse, and Cassius, ran the horserooms. Guys like Hank and Dick at the newsrooms, Doc Cook, and Hymie the Tailor wrote the numbers.

When you played the numbers, for the young or otherwise uninitiated, you selected three digits. The numbers runner would be around in the morning to take your bets. He wrote your name or your code on the top of the slip with the date, then wrote your number, and many people played more than one, on the main part of the slip. He marked down the size of your bet, from a penny to a dollar on the left side of the slip and noted if you "boxed" your number on the right. Boxing the number was playing a cent or two for a payoff if the three digits you played came in, but not in the order you had selected. If you played 123, and the number that day was 231, and you had it boxed, you got a buck back for every penny you played. Straight play paid $6 for a penny, so a dollar on a number would pay $600.

Back to the first two. Midway through the afternoon, you would call either Hank's Newsroom on South Street, or Collins Newsroom on Warren Street and ask for "the first two." If you called too early, they would simply say "not yet." You couldn't rush these things, the first two came in when it came in from the great numbers parlor in the sky, or Albany. Usually the guy answering phones that day would just answer by saying two numbers because there were not many people calling newsrooms at 3 in the afternoon to inquire about cigars.

After getting the magic first two numbers, my next job was to report it to whomever was sitting in the backroom of the market, which at times was a considerable group. Then I had to go next door to the card room and just duck my head into the smoke and say "54," or some such, reporting the first two. If someone around the table had played those numbers and was "alive" for the final, he would usually say, "Here you go, kid," and flip me a nickel out of the pile of money in front of him on the table.

One day Horse Hamlin was playing cards, and he tossed me a nickel, which instead of running down to Kiley's for a Coke, I kept. Next morning I saw Doc Cook on the back of the three-wheel motorcycle collecting nickels from the parking meters with one of the cops, and I told him I wanted to play 256.

"You playing for your dad or yourself?" Doc asked. "For me, Doc, for me, you know my father only plays 257."

It was true. My father had played our house number on Ridge Street, 257, for years. He never won, but he did win a box one day on it for 752.

Doc wrote my policy number on the slip, noted I had bet five cents straight on 256, and asked me if I wanted to box it. I didn't have any other money, so I told him, "No, not today, no need, 256 is gonna win straight." He and the cop laughed, Doc put my slip in his cigar box next to the tray that held the nickel boxes from the parking meters, and they rolled away down South Street.

I called twice and got, "not yets," but when I finally got through about 3 p.m., the old voice I knew so well from daily calls growled "25." I was so nervous I couldn't stand it. I had never called for the final before but knew about 5 p.m. the three numbers from the daily treasury balance came in. "Final, 256," the voice said. I nearly fainted. "Mim mere, mim mere," I called out to my grandmother who was waiting on a customer, "I won the number today."

"Don't give the slip to pere," she said without looking up, "He'll take it to the card game."

Next morning, I paced up and down in front of the store waiting for the motorcycle. It didn't come. I finally walked down to Hank's Newsroom and asked if Doc Cook was around. "He isn't working today," the guy told me, "you got a slip from your grandpa, I'll cash it."

"It's my slip," I said as defiantly as a seven year old can be in a newsroom filled with players. Everyone laughed, but the guy gave me my thirty bucks, a fortune.

At dinner that night my father was a bit cool. He finally said, "I hear you hit the numbers." "Yep," I said keeping my eyes on my plate knowing what was coming next. "Did you play 256?" he asked, smiling just a little.

I just grinned at him. "Damn," he said, "but good for you."

He won on 257 the next week, the day before my birthday, and spent it all on me.

You can't have that kind of family fun playing the lottery!

≈

31

BOB IRVING'S STATEMENT

ა

There used to be two kinds of owners of the mighty thorough-breds that invade Saratoga each August. The old money, playboy types who would breeze into the barn area at 1 a.m. with their companion of the moment, "...to check out the horses," get out of the "BMer," or the Mercedes, or the "Jag" with a bottle of champagne and a paper cup and look into the stalls housing their colts and fillys at the meeting.

Then there were the old line sportsmen. The men of the family were out early in the morning watching the workouts, the women ran a few jumping horses, and they all sat in a box in the clubhouse very near the finish line.

Those groups are fading away and being replaced by corporate farms and corporate training facilities that turn over horses like shares in Amalgamated Horse Do Ltd.

Bob Irving never fit any of these molds. Just as he was a unique conductor on the podium in front of the New York City Ballet Orchestra, he was a unique figure as the owner of racing stock.

"Meet me at the barn about 8," he would say, and if he got there by 9:30 you were lucky. He bought a horse at the Fasig Tipton yearling sales one summer. Silver Mallet made it to the track and was a fair allowance horse. Irving got Angel Cordero to ride for him, and his stable was tiny, but more successful than most one or two horse outfits.

Silver Mallet hit the rail one day and got killed in a race. Irving made good use of his insurance money and got another nag but never did become the success at the track that he was on the podium.

Robert Irving was born in Winchester, England where he began his music studies with piano lessons at six. He later studied cello, organ, and percussion, giving him a tremendous background with a variety of instruments in the orchestra. His major educational focus, however, was in the field of Classics, and he won a scholarship in that field to Winchester College and later to New College, Oxford. During his last year at Oxford, Irving began taking courses at the Royal College of Music as well as continuing his work in Classics.

He completed the regular four-year course at the music school in just two years. He was greatly influenced by conductors at the school, including Sir Malcolm Sargant and the well-known ballet conductor, Constant Lambert. After graduation he spent a summer as an operatic coach at Covent Garden, and that fall he accepted a teaching position back home at Winchester College.

In 1939, young Englishmen were not teaching or playing music, they were fighting the enemy, and young Irving joined the Royal Air Force. He earned two Distinguished Flying Crosses in action against the Germans, and at the end of the war was offered the post as conductor of the BBC Orchestra in Glasgow, Scotland. He accepted, and took on his first orchestra, a position he held for four years.

In 1949, Irving was recommended by Constant Lambert, who was then music director of the famed Sadler's Wells Ballet, for a position as conductor with that company. He took the job, Lambert left, and six months later Irving was music director and his career was blooming.

He made five trips to the United States with Sadler's Wells, and when Leon Barzin left the New York City Ballet Orchestra in 1958, Irving applied and was quickly accepted by George Balanchine.

Balanchine and Irving were two men of common interest, music and dance. Balanchine had great respect for music, and the 20th century's best choreographer always made the music a very important part of every ballet he wrote. Irving, the musician, had deep respect for dance and understood the need for music to support the ballet, without getting in the way.

Balanchine and Irving helped the New York City Ballet grow to become the nation's premier dance company. Irving's contributions to helping ballet and dance were widely recognized, and Martha Graham sought him out to conduct her famous dance company whenever he was available. "Robert Irving puts music under the dancer's feet," Graham said.

Irving had enormous talent, and he was always busy, conducting what most felt was the best ballet orchestra in the world, guest conducting most of the world's better symphony orchestras, writing and conducting for films, for television, "Sleeping Beauty, "Cinderella," and "The Nutcracker," and for the stage, including the Theatre Guild's production of "As You Like It," with Katherine Hepburn in New York.

Critics raved about his conducting, dancers agreed, and Balanchine was pleased to have such a musical talent with his ever-growing New York City Ballet. When he was called "the best ballet conductor in the world today" by Alan Rich, critic for *New York Magazine*, all the insiders agreed.

When Balanchine brought the NYCB to Saratoga, Irving was a long-established star as a conductor. Unlike some of the later conductors and music directors of the Philadelphians, who looked at Saratoga as the unsophisticated boonies, Irving was thrilled with spending July working in Saratoga. He would then schedule August for vacation whenever possible and hang around for the race meeting. He started buying and running horses, and when he gave that up, he was still a fixture at the track during the Saratoga meet.

He was a guest in most of the good boxes in the clubhouse, a must-invite on the party scene and one of the most popular persons on the Saratoga Circuit.

Bob Irving was a character, with his red face that glowed against the white dinner jacket he wore to conduct, and his enormous girth. And he was fun. As a horse player he was not the guy you would ask for his numbers, since he spent more time at the mutual windows than at the cashiers.

Irving became so popular in Saratoga, that Maestro Eugene Ormandy gave him the supreme compliment, inviting him to guest conduct the Philadelphia Orchestra during the August season. Ormandy withheld that invitation from many of the day's leading conductors. No one ever saw Leonard Bernstein in front of the Philadelphians, but Bob Irving had the blessing of the Maestro.

Not content to just guest conduct the orchestra, Irving worked with officials at SPAC, and soon there was a special program each August where the front line strings of the great orchestra were pushed back on the stage, and the Philadelphians were joined by dancers from the New York City Ballet.

The ballet-orchestra program soon became one of the major "hits" of the summer season. When something becomes that accepted, a social event in conjunction with it soon follows. A party after the annual dance/music program was soon a sought-after invite.

During this time there was a major national controversy, as the spokesperson for the National Orange Juice Association, Anita Bryant, was making statements against gays, something that raised the ire of several of the dancers with the New York City Ballet. But they were young and corps dancers for the most part, and were ignored.

This bothered Bob Irving, and at the morning master class and rehearsal for the annual dance/orchestra program, he let it be known that later that evening he would make a "statement" in answer to the Bryant controversy.

The amphitheatre was packed as usual, the program was a great success, and the post performance party was to be held backstage at SPAC. Musicians, a few dancers, hordes of socially correct Saratoga types and assorted politicos and hangers-on were drinking the bubbly, eating the finger food and noting how wonderful it was that Saratoga had both the New York City Ballet and the Philadelphia Orchestra, when Bob Irving appeared, having changed out of his dinner jacket and tux pants into a t-shirt and jeans.

The message on the bright orange T-shirt was spread across his barrel chest and huge belly: "Anita Bryant" it said, "sucks oranges."

ء

32

GENE AND HIS BAND

ðÞ

There is some argument— but only from those protecting a band from their own town: Boston, New York, Berlin, or some over-achiever yuppies from Los Angeles—but among those who really know, the Philadelphia Orchestra is the "best band in the land."

The reason the Philadelphians are the best, is because most of them were selected for the chairs in which they sit and play by the best band leader in the world, Eugene Ormandy.

Ormandy, a violinist born in Budapest, was brought to Philadelphia in 1936 to rescue a symphony orchestra that had seen better days. He stayed until 1980, the longest tenure of any major orchestra conductor. He remained as conductor laureate from his retirement as music director in 1980 until his death in 1985 at the age of 86.

His legacy is an orchestra filled with some of the finest individual players of their instruments in the world, but more important, 105 chairs filled with musicians who look forward to, and have the ability to play together.

"Is there a Philadelphia Sound, Maestro?" we asked him one morning after a very difficult rehearsal. "You ask me?" he said, "You sit out there every night, you listen, you tell me."

We both laugh. The Philadelphia Sound is Eugene Ormandy. It is not there all the time, it comes to the fore when there is a piece of music where the strings cut loose. Where Norman Carol, Bill dePasquale, and David Arben lead the first violins, and Luis Biava and Bobby dePasquale boot up the second violins, and Joe dePasquale and his buddies Jim Fawcett and Sidney Curtis spark the violas, and Bill Stokking the cellos, and Rog Scott the bass players. When all this enormous talent comes together, they create what anyone with any kind of ear can identify as the Philadelphia Sound.

Each of these string stars was selected for the Philadelphia Orchestra by Ormandy. He knew what he wanted to hear, he found the people who could play that way, and he filled the orchestra sections with great players. Then he spent decades playing the kind of music people wanted to hear, traditional music by traditional composers.

There was much talk about the world of music having passed Ormandy by, of his lack of appreciation for "modern" music, of playing too much "old, romantic music." His answer was full houses at the Academy of Music in Philadelphia, large crowds at the summer residence in Saratoga, an endless string of international tours, including a blockbuster to China, and more record sales than any other symphony orchestra.

Ormandy was perfect for Saratoga, but it was not the Maestro and the Philadelphians that Nelson Rockefeller and the Saratoga group had in mind when they decided to build the 5,000 seat amphitheatre and its sloping lawns in the 1960s. Rockefeller wanted the New York Philharmonic to come to Saratoga for the summer, and when they hesitated the Philadelphians were invited, and Ormandy became the music director for the building of Saratoga Performing Arts Center.

While George Balanchine designed the stage floor, with its battleship linoleum, Ormandy designed the sound. While the amphitheatre is open on the sides, when you stand on the stage and look out at the cavern of seats and the long stretches of lawns, the sound baffles on the sides make it appear to be closed in on both sides. An Ormandy plan.

There was a problem about the sound reaching the lawn. Sound is slow, and the music played on the stage is heard a fraction of a second later on the lawn than by those in the seats, and there was need to give some amplification to the sound to reach the lawns. Problem! The amplified sound got to the lawn crowd before the natural sound. Solution! Record the natural sound at the rear of the amphitheatre, delay it for a fraction, then pour it out to the lawn crowd. Hardly anyone knows they are hearing a combination of natural and amplified sound, since both arrive at your ears at the same time when you sit on your blanket and sip the horrible New York State wines they sell at the little carts.

As work progressed on the amphitheatre and plans were made for the opening during the summer of 1966, Ormandy visited the site. "What is that awful noise?" he asked, "did someone flush all the toilets?" No, the running water Ormandy heard was the creek that flows through Saratoga Geyser Park as it has for centuries. "Not acceptable," Ormandy said, "turn off the water."

In today's stricter environmental atmosphere, Ormandy would have had to pick up his two harps, Mike Bookspan's drums, and left for a summer festival in Washington. But in 1966, workmen "turned off the water." A dam was built, and when the Maestro or a guest conductor strode on stage at 8:15 p.m. for a concert, the water was shut off. As the final notes sound and applause echoes through the rafters annoying the birds who annoy the patrons, the dam is opened, and the water gushes through until another concert begins.

Ormandy brought the Saratoga audience along slowly, performing plenty of traditional music during the first few seasons. He brought in an exciting array of guest conductors, but carefully controlled who he let take over his great orchestra. The Maestro was in charge of the Philadelphians. He selected the musicians, he selected the guest soloists, he selected the guest conductors, he selected the music. It was the Eugene Ormandy show.

Ormandy was no stranger to summer programs. He first conducted the Philadelphia Orchestra in the summer of 1930 at Robin Hood Dell outside Philadelphia. His performance with the orchestra impressed the board, and he was given a shot on the podium on October 25, 1931, in the Philadelphia Academy of Music, replacing an ailing Arturo Toscanini.

He then took on the job as music director of the Minneapolis Symphony, remaining there from 1931 to 1936. When the job at Philadelphia opened, he was the first choice of the board who remembered his excellent work of five years before.

During his long tenure with the Philadelphians he became a legend. He was one of the last full-time conductors. He looked askance at the "gypsy" conductors of the day who traveled the world with baton in hand, leading every band in every town. "I am very happy in Philadelphia," he said. He turned down countless offers and stayed with his beloved Philadelphians, carefully selected the musician he wanted for every seat, took a few guest jobs each year in New York and with the Boston band near his summer home at Tanglewood.

Trumpet player Frank Kaderabek had paid his dues in Detroit and was recognized as one of the very best symphonic trumpet virtuosos in the world. He had a call to New York, Boston wanted him. Ormandy listened, and said yes. Kaderabek has been principal trumpet with the Philadelphians for years.

The same was true in other sections as players accepted the bid to come to Philadelphia, to be one of Ormandy's men. Anthony Gigliotti, principal clarinet, the smooth-playing Glenn Dodson, principal trombone, and many others created, with the super-powerful string sections, the Philadelphia Sound.

Ormandy had a worsening problem with his hip, something he thought he had to live with until medical science discovered the miracle of replacing the hip. Ormandy left the podium for a season to have the operation and recover, and the summer season at Saratoga was not the same.

The orchestra that thrived on its discipline, on tight sound, on perfection, was not the same. Norman Carol, with the magic sounds of his violin in the concertmaster's chair, had a mysterious ailment cripple his hand. The sound was different. Many ignored it, they were still better than the rest. My reviews that summer were harsh, noting the band lacked concentration, discipline, and were not performing up to the skills that were in the chairs.

The recording director sent me a note to come into the recording room after rehearsal. "Bravo, bravo," the old man who had listened to the Philadelphians through his headset for every note they had played for years said. "Give them hell, the old men know you mean well, the young men are angry, but they are not playing well. Discipline, discipline, say it again and again."

By the end of the season most of them wouldn't speak to me. The next summer, Ormandy was back, new hip, same old attitude.

He had his favorite pianist with him for opening night, Andre Watts. After the morning rehearsal, he sent his valet to bring me back. "You asked me years ago if there is a Philadelphia Sound.

I read what you wrote last year when I was gone. Thank God you have learned what is good, what is right. Listen tonight."

That evening the crowd cheered itself hoarse when he walked to the podium, no limp, straight, strong. He turned to the crowd and waved his stick, together they sang the national anthem of his adopted country. Even in that tough piece of music it was obvious: The sound, the Maestro, and the band were back.

ₔ

33

DINERS ARE DIFFERENT

੩♦

I like diners. But they have to be real diners.

A real diner is a place where a guy in a well worn apron says, "What'll you have?" You tell him, and he cooks it for you on a grill.

Those fancy, dancy diners where there is a menu with 1,000 items, a disclaimer, "No Substitutions" and the food is a pouch tossed into boiling water or a microwave in the kitchen, are not diners.

In a diner the grill guy cooks your eggs, home fries, and ham on the grill, along with the guy on the next stool's pancakes and two egg sandwiches to go for the cabbie at the register, while he talks to the entire counter about baseball, politics, women, and the price of butter.

Diners have good coffee, pies that have never seen the inside of a freezer, greasy donuts, corn muffins that break into 34 pieces when you try to butter them, and hard rolls toasted on a grill held down by the plate on which they will serve it to you.

Coffee in a diner comes from a huge stainless steel urn, not some little glass pot. If you take cream in your coffee, they slap a metal do jiggy that lets just the right amount out into the big thick cup. They don't serve those little plastic boxes filled with soy drippings and call it cream. You take sugar? Turn the glass shaker upside down and let the sugar pour into your cup, no little paper packets.

Diners are places where people say hello, thank you, and never "Have a nice day." Diners are filled with truck drivers, cabbies, cops, and those who realize good fast food does not come from fast food joints, but from a grill behind a counter from a guy who has flipped more hamburgers than Wendy himself.

There have been a number of good diners in this area, the most famous being the Palace Lunch on Warren Street in Glens Falls. The front door of the Palace did not open in or out, it slid to one side. Once inside you found a row of old black stools that started at the door and went down a long counter to the back. There was just enough room to walk behind the stools, hang up your coat on an old iron hook and slide into a seat at the counter. The counter was heavy glass, and under it sat pies, cakes, muffins, and other assorted items that came up from the kitchen deep underneath the little diner. Coffee was served in a thick, white ceramic cup. Some of the cups had names written on them of long gone—and except for the cups—forgotten diners of the past. Milk came in a glass that weighed half a pound.

There was no menu, but there were specials, and they were written down somewhere, but the regulars knew what was planned each day. Wednesday was meatloaf, Saturday and Sunday were chicken pie, but Thursday was "shucks and balls." For 85 cents you would get a good-sized bowl of what today is called "pasta," and two meatballs, covered with a rich, red sauce. There would be a couple slices of Italian bread, a glop of soft butter on the side, and a shaker of grated cheese. A soda would come in one of the huge, thick glasses poured out of a bottle. The counterman would pop the top off the soda using an opener screwed onto the wall. A container below the wall opener was meant to catch the falling caps, but by mid-day it would be full and there would be a pile of caps on the floor.

The artist who cuts my hair, Joe DiVivo, and his long-time partner Phil DeAngelo, used to walk around the corner to the Palace from the barbershop for lunch. They still talk about "shucks and balls" like it was last Thursday when we had them, and not 20 years or more ago.

There was a cast of characters in the Palace who felt it was their place to know every customer and be able to insult him where it hurt most. You were a cop, they knew about the unlocked door on his beat he had missed. You were a bus driver, they knew about the old lady who had complained you had stopped the bus too quick, and she had nearly fallen down. You were a lawyer, they knew how you screwed up your last case in

City Court, and since the judges ate there as well, they were just as fair game as the lawyers.

Mert came to the Palace when he was a teenager. He moved from the last few stools up the row toward the door very quickly. Mert was a born counterman, and became a good businessman. After the Palace became an urban renewal waste dump, its cups crushed by the bulldozers in the rubble of its cellar, Mert opened his own place on Glen Street and made blueberry muffins an art form.

Tucker was another one who started when he was just old enough to get working papers, and he grew with the place as well. Tuck later had his own place on Glen Street, but it didn't last as long as Mert's.

Hap was a character. Despite his name, there was a certain sadness about Happy, but he kept a running patter with most of the regulars. One election night Hap called Fred Carota at the radio station and asked if he wanted a story. "Not tonight, it's elections," the harried newscaster told him. "Well, I'm gonna jump off the bridge anyway," Hap said. And he did!

But the main character in the Palace was Earl. He was born to be a counterman. If you were making a movie or a TV series and it needed a counterman, Earl O'Connor was your man. A long-ago white apron tied about his bony frame, a paper lunch cart hat off at an angle, faster than Superman himself at the grill.

Earl was a short order cook, a grillman par excellent. No one could touch him at his trade. Eggs, burgers, westerns, easterns, omelets, muffins, potatoes, name it, Earl could spin it onto and off his grill, cooked to your liking.

He handled most of the front stools, the grill, the cash register, and answered the phone. Cops did not carry those Dick Tracy radios they now have when the go for coffee, they told the desk sergeant they were going to the Palace from a call box in Bank Square, and if they were needed, the desk guy would call them. Usually Earl would just take the call. "There's a fire on Lawrence Street," he would tell the car man, taking back the half-eaten hamburger that would get finished later. "Bank alarm, First National," he would tell the beat cop, putting his pie under the glass of the case.

He was also protective of his regulars. One night after closing down the newspaper, we wandered in for pie and coffee. The phone rings, Earl mumbles a few words and covers the speaker:

"You here?" he asks. "It's your bride, something about the house being filled with smoke. I can send the car man," he said, nodding toward the cop on the end stool.

"No," I said, "this one I should take myself." When I got to the door he had wrapped my pie and put the coffee into a container. "No need to waste this," he said. Thankfully it was only a plastic bowl that had fallen onto the dryer element of the dish washer.

WWSC, the local radio station, was located on the second floor of the building next door to the Palace. You could come out a back door of the main control room, go down the fire escape, climb onto the Palace back porch and get into the end of the diner, where a counter guy would get you a "coffee to go for the radio," and something to eat. You could do this during the four minutes and thirty seconds the network fed the news or during a long record.

Bob Jennings, "BJ the DJ" came in one night, they whisked him his coffee and pie, and he disappeared into the darkness climbing back up the fire escape. The door had closed, and you couldn't open it from the outside. BJ was alone in the station playing records, and the one on the turntable was about to end.

He flew down the fire escape, over the rail and into the back door of the diner. To get to the front door, you had to go along the tiny area where the counter guys worked, but there was no way hefty BJ was going to get past three countermen. He let out a whoop that chased all three of the Palace crew out the door to make way for him to get to the street. BJ ran down to the door to the station, which of course was locked. His keys, upstairs in his coat.

The cop in Bank Square heard him yelling and went over, broke the glass with his nightstick and got BJ up the stairs to the record, which was long over.

The other local eating spot of diner quality was the Glens Falls Diner on South Street. It was more of a restaurant, and the German folks who ran it later sold out and opened the Ridge Terrace, a nice restaurant on Ridge Road near Kattskill Bay. A treat after a basketball game was to take your best girl to the Diner for French fries and a coke. One huge plate of fries, two Cokes and two forks, and a buck covered it and the tip.

There were lots of neighborhood diners, every section of town had its own. The one that remains is Poopies on Lawrence

Street. Poopie DiManno ran it as a neighborhood diner, where you could also put a bob or two on a racing nag as well. In later years his son, Jerry, himself a character in his own right, remodeled the place, put in a new grill and now runs a genuine diner where you stand in line for a seat at breakfast or lunch. Get there by 2 p.m., because that's when they close, and order a Poopieburger, because it is the only place in the world where they are served.

ਣਾ

34

I BROKE IT

Maestro Eugene Ormandy had his favorite musicians whom he liked to have perform as soloists with the Philadelphia Orchestra. None were more popular with the legendary conductor than pianist Andre Watts.

Ormandy had first heard Watts play as a child when he won the 1957 Philadelphia Orchestra Children's Audition. In 1962, Watts, who had been studying at the Philadelphia Music Academy, got an opportunity to perform as a soloist with the New York Philharmonic at one of Leonard Bernstein's now famous Young People's Concerts. The 16 year old played so well that Bernstein called him two weeks later to substitute for the often-ailing Glenn Gould at a regular Philharmonic subscription concert.

This launched his international career, and for the past 30 years, Watts has been performing with about every major orchestra in the world.

He made his European debut at 20 with the London Symphony in 1966, and a year later was guest soloist with the Berlin Symphony. The U.S. State Department had him make a world tour in 1967, and it was very successful.

Watts was born in Nuremberg, Germany, the son of a black American GI and his Hungarian wife. He started playing violin at the age of four, but quickly switched to piano. His mother provided him lessons, then when he improved and was obviously going to be very talented, started taking lessons from a number of outstanding teachers.

He was the guest soloist on the first PBS broadcast of the TV series "Live from Lincoln Center" in 1976 and performed the first full-length piano recital in the history of television.

Watts was almost a regular with Ormandy in appearing with the Philadelphia Orchestra to open the summer seasons at Saratoga Performing Arts Center. Each August he would be on the opening night bill, assuring a good crowd, because he had become very popular with Saratoga audiences.

So when the Philadelphia Orchestra Guild and a group of Saratoga orchestra supporters purchased a new concert grand piano from Steinway and Sons and presented it to be used for concerts at SPAC, Ormandy immediately selected Watts to play the dedication concert.

The concert on Wednesday, August 10, 1977, was to open the 12th season of the Philadelphians at the Saratoga Festival. It was raining, but the house was still quite full. It was the season opener, Watts was the soloist, Ormandy was to conduct, and scores of patrons who had donated to the purchase of the new piano were on hand.

The Steinway representatives were nervous, since this was not just another sale of a piano, this was to be the concert grand to be used by some of the world's great players with one of the world's finest orchestras at a summer festival, with the highest of visibility in a town filled with celebrities for every orchestra/ track season.

The Steinway grand that had been used in concerts was put in the rehearsal hall behind the stage, and the new piano was on the side of the stage for the official dedication concert. Watts was to perform in the second half of the evening, after the orchestra had played the first half. During the intermission, the Steinway people watched nervously as the SPAC stage crew and the Philadelphia Orchestra stage hands brought the grand piano to center stage. It was positioned to the left, as seen by the audience, of Ormandy's specially built conducting stand.

Watts led Ormandy onto the stage, and a roar of applause greeted the two musicians. Watts always had a special affinity for Ormandy, feeling the Maestro had been one of the prime movers in what was a very successful career as a concert pianist. Watts had often told interviewers and friends playing with the Philadelphians and Ormandy was exciting, but performing with them at Saratoga was, "very, very special to me."

Ormandy took to the podium, Watts nodded he was ready, and the great orchestra began the dedication concert of its new piano. Watts is a powerful player, he gives each performance full measure of his talents, and he was flailing away when suddenly the pedal assembly of the new piano flew off and scattered on the stage.

Watts jumped up from his seat on the bench, looked under the piano, saw the pedal box on the floor and immediately dropped to his hands and knees and crawled under the huge concert grand.

Ormandy, conducting the orchestra with his back to Watts, had seen none of this show. Then, realizing he was not hearing the piano, he turned to look at the guest soloist and nearly dropped his baton when he saw the piano bench was empty. He was to say later, "I could not imagine where Andre was. Players just don't get up and leave in the middle of a performance. I was worried he had become ill."

Watts was ill, he was distraught. He crawled around on the stage picking up pieces of the piano, which he carried off stage to the wings.

Standing in the wings were several of the people who had raised money to purchase the new piano, terrified representatives of Steinway, and, nearest the stage, the wife of a local critic. Walking up to her, Watts said, "Look, look," holding out the broken pedal assembly, "I broke it." She tried to reassure him he had not broken the new piano, as the Steinway people just kept backing away, not wanting to accept the fact the expensive new concert grand was falling apart with the Philadelphia Orchestra and Eugene Ormandy on the stage and 5,000 people in the amphitheatre.

Ormandy had stopped the band with a wave, and the audience, most of whom could not see what had happened to the piano, only that Watts had stood up and then crawled away under the piano, was buzzing.

Ormandy quickly joined Watts off stage and looked in amazement at the collection of pedal parts in the piano player's hands. "What happened?" he asked Watts. "Gene," the shaken player said, "I think I broke it."

The situation suddenly became so bizzare, that Ormandy, Watts, and the woman they had stopped to talk with all broke out in laughter. The Steinway people did not join in the fun.

Ormandy slapped Watts on the back and told him,"Andre you did not break this piano, let's see what happened."

An inspection of the piano by the Steinway people revealed that when the new grand had been unloaded at Saratoga, the technicians from Steinway and Sons had not finished putting in the screws that hold the pedal assembly to the bottom of the piano. The entire assembly was held in place by transport screws, and when Watts started playing the instrument, the few screws had come loose and the pedal assembly had gone flying across the SPAC stage.

"Where's the old piano?" Ormandy asked no one in particular. "I think it's in the rehearsal hall," someone on the stage replied. "Get it," Ormandy ordered the Steinway folks, "and get that one off my stage," he said waving at the pedal-less concert grand sitting in front of the now-laughing orchestra.

The new piano was rolled away. The old piano was resurrected from the hall and moved to center stage. Watts came out and tried a few bars, said it was OK, and Ormandy returned to the podium.

Before the Maestro could crank up the band and Watts could go back to the keyboard, the audience stood as one and gave them all an ovation.

Ormandy went to the beginning of the second movement, Watts started playing, a bit tentatively at first, but soon he was immersed in the music, beating up the old Steinway, which poured forth great sounds.

Watts has returned to Saratoga many times since the 1977 season opener, and he has become one of the brightest stars on the concert scene in the world. But whenever he sees the woman he first met in the wings that night several years ago, he always laughs, cradles his arms, and instead of hello says, "I broke it."

ᏃᏘ

35

COLD SODA NEEDS ICE

ᴣᴀ

Did you ever drink a Moxie?

If you did you would remember it. Moxie was a soft drink that was around when soda pop came in glass bottles. It had what we shall call a "unique" taste. If you think Dr. Pepper is different, square that and add a few to the result, and you have the taste of Moxie.

There were actually people who drank it on a regular basis. Not enough, however, as you don't see it much anymore, if ever. But that's enough.

I am addicted to soda pop, and thought the best thing my grand-pere ever did in his meat market was to put in a cooler and start selling cold soda. The first cooler was a metal monster that stood on legs and had a fold-back top. You could open one side of the top over onto the other to look for your favorite flavor of soda that would be nestled down under a few buckets of shaved Hovey Pond ice.

If the ice didn't come up over the top of the bottles it was easy to see what flavors were in the cooler, since the cap told you: "Grape," "Birch Beer," "Cream Soda," "Pineapple," "Fruit Punch," "Cherry," and even "Ginger Ale," but I think my grand-pere kept that in there for himself and used it to mix with the bottle of Four Roses he kept in the cooler in the pickle barrel.

As soon as the soda cooler had been brought into the store, my mother set up rules about my not swilling soda, and put my grand-mere in charge of making sure I did not go over my quota. I figured if grand-pere could get a few snorts from the booze he had stashed in the cooler, I would just put a few extra bottles of soda in there and work off that supply.

It worked for a few days, but one hot afternoon I went to grab a cold grape and found no soda in my hiding place. One afternoon in the truck when we were delivering orders to customers grand-pere asked me, "Did she find your soda too?" I guess that meant she found his Four Roses in the pickles.

The ice man would come every morning. He would have huge cakes of ice on his truck, which he would break into smaller pieces and put through the grinder on the back of the truck. He would catch the crushed ice in the bucket and lug it into the store for the meat cases, dropping a couple of buckets in the soda case.

On hot summer days the ice would melt, and I remember having to scoop some out of the meat cases and drop it into the soda cooler about 3, so there would be cold soda for customers until we closed up at 6.

One day a truck pulled up and brought in a bright red cooler. It had "Coca Cola" written all over it in white letters. The guys who brought it ran a hose from the back room sink where we cleaned chickens and washed the hamburg grinder parts and filled the new cooler with water. They plugged it into a wall outlet near the door, and a pump started circulating water inside the cooler.

There was a refrigerating unit in the pump, and soon the water was cold. We had stopped getting ice for the meat cases because they had become refrigerated, and now the ice man had no reason to stop anymore.

The first warm day I complained to grand-pere the soda wasn't as cold as when we had ice and he explained it was cold enough, he was saving on buying ice, and since he started carrying Coke as well as the other flavors, the Coke bottler had provided the new electric cooler free for the store.

"This is progress," he explained. "The cooler has advertising all over it, it makes people think to buy a soda, and we don't have to buy ice." I reminded him he was paying Niagara Mohawk for the electricity, but he said that was cheaper than buying ice, he thought.

The soda in the old cooler had come from Ray's Beverages, a local bottling plant on Woodward Avenue. The new cooler still had Ray's, which came in a clear bottle that held about eight ounces, and also those little fat, green bottles of coke. One day a guy came to see grand pere and tried to get him to put Hires root beer in the case. He gave me a bottle and it was great, the best root beer I had ever tasted. "Get it, Pip," I told him, "that's great soda." He scowled at me and told me to go put up orders.

Later he explained he couldn't put Hires in the cooler, and he was lucky the Coke guys were letting him keep Ray's. Time passed, and two, and later three coolers were in the market. We had Pepsi, Mission orange, and lots of other flavors and brands, including one case of Moxie that lasted for months.

My group never knew buying cold soda out of an ice-filled cooler or even taking one from the circulating water. They grew up in an era when soda was dispensed from machines in cans, or bottles were offered in a cooler where you opened the door, took one off a shelf and another slid down to take its place.

One day my friend Bodie Hallenbeck came walking up to the side door of our house. The kids went out to meet him and he waited until all of them had gathered. "Watch," he said, taking a bottle of Pepsi out of a bag. He tossed it into the air, and it landed on the concrete sidewalk with a plop. The kids were quick to point out the bottle didn't break, since it was plastic.

Bodie's son Chris, a marketing guy for Pepsico, was bringing out this new package, a plastic soda bottle. It was the end of an era, but the beginning of another.

Gone were the days of searching for the famous green Coke bottles that had fallen over in the cooler. Searching for the red, white, and blue logo of the Pepsi bottle. No pulling an ice-cold bottle from the ice, watching it break out into a sweat from the heat of the day and hearing it sizzle with foam in a glass filled with ice you took from the case.

The colder you could get the soda, the better the flavor, especially with the root beer and the orange, although a frosty grape could cut a thirst on a July afternoon.

All of this is now just a distant memory in a time when more soda is sold from dispensers in a paper cup than from bottles, and they try to sell you three-liter jugs that don't even fit inside your refrigerator, and the soda goes flat before you finish it anyway.

I have long lamented the passing of the old metal coolers and the modernization of soda pop, which is one of America's few contributions to the beverage scene. However, arriving at the Lake George house one day, I found this old red and white metal Coke cooler sitting on the upper part of the deck. The top was held down by a springy metal handle that closed up over the entire top. I sprung it back, lifted the top, and inside was a sea of crushed ice. Bottles of soda lay buried in the chips.

"How do you like my cooler?" one of the twins asked. "I found it at a garage sale. You know Dad, soda gets colder, and you won't believe this, but it tastes better when you keep it in ice. Try one."

I sat there in the old rocker looking at the mountains, sipping a frosty soda, chuckling to myself. "What's so funny?" the oldest girl asked.

"Nothing, nothing. Get a soda out of that old cooler and sit here for a while."

ра

36

WINGS/GLENS/GLENN'S/ HOMETOWN FALLS

જ

You can get a lot of free beers on this trivia question: How many names has Glens Falls been known by since Abraham Wing set up shop by the river?

Anyone with any sense of history about this place, Glens Falls, knows it was first named for the Quaker Abraham Wing who cleared a small portion of land and started a community. Being a person of no small pride, he called it Wing's Falls. But, as the book says, pride goeth before the falls.

Wing ran a tavern in what is today Bank Square, and one evening he hosted a card game/party. Among the revelers was a Colonel John Glen. When Wing ran out of coin, he offered, so the story goes, the name of the town to the pot, which Glen won.

Next day, Glen had his men putting up handbills noting the community would henceforth be known as Glen's Falls. Wing plotted to get Glen into another game, this time with his deck, but fate and the Iroquois intervened. Glen lost his scalp to a French raiding party, and old Abe never did get an opportunity to put his name back on the welcome sign.

During the years, Glen's became Glens, and for nearly two centuries the name marked the hamlet, later village, and in 1908 the city by the falls of the Hudson River.

James Fenimore Cooper was passing over the bridge, another story goes, when he was taken down and shown a hole in the rocks where the water had eaten its way through, thousands of years before. Cooper saw the possibility of making something of this "cave," especially in historically conscious England, and he made it a big part of his novel, *The Last of the Mohicans*. Many felt the town should make note of Cooper's Cave being here but Cooperstown to the west beat them to the name.

As the space program took off and captured the imagination of the populace, and Colonel John Glenn went into space, a local newspaper reporter convinced the Common Council to re-name the city "Glenn's Orbits" for 24 hours, as Colonel Glenn whirled around overhead. The Council voted unanimously, the only thing Tom Marzola and Bill Mangine agreed on all year, to give the city the name for a day to honor the astronaut.

So those are the three official names of the place. Now for the nickname, "Hometown U.S.A.," which was given to Glens Falls by *Look* Magazine in 1943. There are as many poorly researched stories about this as there are writers who think they found something new. There have been stories that the nickname was because of a story in the *Saturday Evening Post*, or because of a series published in *Life* Magazine. Neither is true.

The editors of *Look* Magazine, at the Curtis Publishing Company in Philadelphia, came up with a great idea. Find a typical American community, everyone's "hometown," and provide pictures and stories about it to American GIs scattered all over Europe and Asia fighting two World Wars.

Glens Falls was selected, was dubbed "Hometown U.S.A.," and *Look* sent a bevy of photographers here to record life in Glens Falls. Several of the shooters were here nearly all of 1943, taking pictures for the series that would run the next year. The series began with the April 4, 1944 issue of *Look* and continued in five more issues wrapping up in the issue of November 28, 1944.

While most of the photographs were black and white, the *Look* staff also took more than 2,000 color slides of life in the Glens Falls area. These were to be used to select covers for *Look*.

The series was an editorial success. Life as it went on at home was recorded in pictures and story, and the soldiers, sailors, Marines, and U.S. Army Air Corps guys and gals around the world reacted just as *Look* editors had hoped they would.

Glens Falls put up signs "Hometown U.S.A." and the name was used by the Chamber of Commerce and others to promote the location well after the end of World War II.

The boxes and boxes of color slides were sent back to Philadelphia and stored in the Curtis archives. Perhaps one was used, but the big push for a color cover to illustrate the stories lost out to other stories and other pictures.

Time passes and so did Curtis, going out of business. An editor at Curtis had an old friend in Glens Falls, Arthur P. Irving, publisher of *The Post-Star* and *The Glens Falls Times*. As Curtis was fading from the scene, the editor packed the Glens Falls slides in boxes and shipped them to Irving in Glens Falls. A creature of habit, Art Irving kept all the mail, notes, messages, and packages that had arrived during the day in one place. At the end of the day, it was all wrapped into a newspaper of that day and kept.

As AP's office and files were being examined following his death in 1982, the collection of color slides showing Glens Falls in 1943 were re-discovered. The Irving family donated them to Crandall Library, and a program to make a slide show from the thousands of slides was begun. A great number of people spent a great deal of time viewing the slides, making identifications and selecting two trays, about 160 slides, for a show. Many people were brought to the Crandall Library auditorium to look at slides and identify the people shown. Retired teachers, retired cops, and old-time politicians were the ones who recognized the most.

After the show had been selected, we wrote a script that is updated whenever the slides are shown, refining the identifications, putting more names to faces.

The slides are a unique collection of people and places. There are parades with the Second Regiment Band, a collection of old and young musicians, all the rest were away at war. Pictures of homes, neighborhoods, churches, and lots of people. Every place in America had scrap drives during the War, but Glens Falls is one of the few places where the collection of newspapers for the war effort is documented in color photos.

There are pictures of kids riding bikes, and women pushing carriages, of cops directing traffic outside the high school, of swimming at Round Pond and East Field's quarry pond.

The *Look* photographers had documented a community at a point in time, just as they had been mandated to do. While most of the photos were never seen by the soldiers in Europe and the islands of the Pacific, the shooters had kept an era alive in the collection.

The emergence of the slide show and its showing to scores of groups made the old name Hometown U.S.A. popular once again. The slogan became a source of pride in the community and gave it great identity.

There have been a variety of stories about why Glens Falls was selected over all the small cities throughout the United States as the typical American hometown. Local pride would have itthat it was because nowhere else in the country reflected how hometown America handled the war as well as Glens Falls. A nice idea. *Look's* editorial board helped that idea along, issuing a statement when they announced that Glens Falls had been selected as their target city: "Glens Falls contains in microcosm, every aspect of the American Ideal, every potential for achievement of the American Ideal."

One thing that did amaze *Look's* editors was that 3,000 of the 19,000 residents of the Greater Glens Falls area were in the armed forces during World War II.

However, a few years ago, an old employee of Curtis, long retired, remembered a different reason for the Upstate New York selection.

During World War II, there was no color film available to the public, it all went to the Signal Corps for military photos. Curtis wanted to shoot the Hometown U.S.A. project in four color as well as black and white, and went to the War Department seeking help.

The Secretary of War got involved in the project, and it was made known to Curtis' executives that there might be a supply of color slide film available for such a fine, patriotic project if the Secretary's hometown was given a bit of consideration. Secretary of War Robert Patterson had grown up in a little place called Glens Falls. Glens Falls, New York, a perfect Hometown U.S.A.

ᴥ

37

FIRST TIME AT SARATOGA

ಌ

It was one of those quiet mid-week afternoons at the Saratoga meeting. There was no stakes race on the card, it was hot, and there was more talk than writing in the press box.

Red Smith was still the dean of the coop high above the end of the stretch at Saratoga. He would spin yarns about the days when he was in this box with the likes of Damon Runyon, Grantland Rice, Jim Bishop —who was still doing sports and not historical novels— and steeds like Whirlaway, Greentree's Devil Diver, C.V. Whitney's Top Flight, War Admiral, Eight Thirty, and the great handicap older horse Discovery were running in circles at Saratoga.

Everyone at Saratoga has memories. There was an old writer from the *Troy Record* who would be asked every year to recount the running of the 1919 Sanford when Upset handed Man 'o War his only defeat. Several regulars could still remember the 1930 Travers, when Jim Dandy went off at 100 to 1 and beat the odds-on favorite Gallant Fox.

In later years, our group would be asked by newcomers to talk about the 1973 Whitney, when the unknown Onion ran down Triple Crown champion Secretariat, or the great Affirmed finished first in the 1978 Travers and was disqualified and placed second to his chief rival Alydar, as the biggest crowd in Saratoga history looked on.

Saratoga is built on stories, and everyone has their own memories. This quiet afternoon talk got around to the first time writers in the coop had been to Saratoga. Smith had been a young reporter from New York, a couple of guys from the Racing Form had first seen the track as assistants to the chart writers.

"How about you home boy?" Joe Hirsch, the columnist from the *Form* asked me. "You grew up here, you must have seen this place early." "Not too early," I told him. "I walked hots at the trotters (Saratoga Raceway up the street on Nelson Avenue) but I didn't get in here until I was a teen-ager, but I sure do remember the day."

"I hope it's a horse story," Jim McCulley who had written for the *Daily News* for 50 years said.

"It is," I told him, "you'll like this one."

During the summer of 1952, baseball held out more to me than horses, but one August morning it was raining, no baseball. My cousin, Ken Usher, Jr., called, and asked if I would like to go to Saratoga to the races. I had been around the track, I had an aunt who had a place on Saratoga Lake, and I knew I couldn't visit her in August, because she rented the place to a trainer who had a string at Saratoga.

We got there in time for the daily double, and I remember I was alive after the first race, but my pick in the second finished "up the track," as some guy who stood near us at the rail noted. This guy was obviously a horse player, so I listened to him during the afternoon. He didn't win, but he talked a good scheme.

The horses came out for the feature race, it was the 50th running of the Saratoga Special, a sweepstakes where the winner takes all. I was impressed by this handsome gray horse. This horse looked strong, and his rider, a guy named Eric Guerin, looked like he was in complete control.

The Saratoga Special is a six-furlong sprint for two-year-old colts, so there wasn't much information on the careers of the runners, since they were just babies starting their careers on the dirt.

I noticed in the program that Guerin had won the Saratoga Special the year before with a horse named Cousin. I was with my cousin, wasn't that a sign?

I talked a lot about this gray horse, and the wise guy by the rail turned and said to me: "Kid, let me give you some good advice. Never bet on gray horses. Gray horses don't run good."

He should know, but I did like the looks of that horse. When my cousin went to bet, I sent along $2, "to win."

Six-furlong sprints start way across the track, so standing by the rail in front of the grandstand, you don't get much of a view of the start. I heard Fred Caposella announce, "They're off," and I listened intently for any mention of my choice. When the field came down the long stretch, I could see the cerise and white diamond colors of the Alfred G. Vanderbilt Stable, and they were in front of all the others.

Guerin just rode him home and had back-to-back wins in the Saratoga Special. The wise guy told me it was a fluke, to remember that gray horses were never a good bet. "Look at that time," he said pointing to the infield timer. I didn't know if 1:13.1 was good or bad. I learned later it was pretty good for the shape the track was in, even though it was about two seconds slower than the time posted in the "Special" by Battleship a couple of years earlier.

"Look at the odds, 13-1, this was a fluke," the tout at the rail told me. "That gray horse is nothin." I thought $28 for my bet was something, and come to find out that horse was a lot more than "nothin."

That horse was a champion named Native Dancer and was certainly a gray horse to bet, although he never paid much again. Native Dancer and Eric Guerin went on to win and win, including the 1953 Travers at Saratoga. In 1963, Native Dancer was inducted into the Racing Hall of Fame.

Years later, when I was covering this sport, I was at the 1972 induction ceremonies at the Hall of Fame. Among those inducted that day was a jockey named Eric Guerin. As the group of writers gathered about Guerin drifted away, I told him the story of the gray horse, and the advice the railbird had given me.

"He sure was a great one, wasn't he?" the little man smiled. "He beat me into this place by nine years, but I can't kick. Having been his rider is one of the reasons I'm here at all. I would never have made the Hall of Fame without Native Dancer.

"We all know the gray horse story," Guerin mused, "but sometimes gray horses do run good."

I knew they had liked my story in the Saratoga press box when I read it in two newspapers the next day as columns.

❧

38

BARYSHNIKOV

George Balanchine had a hard and fast rule in his New York City Ballet company: No stars. The great choreographer felt there were three classes of dancers in his troupe: the youngsters who danced in the corps, those who graduated to become soloists, and the best, who became principals.

Balanchine ran his company on a no-star basis, even though many of his dancers did reach star stature outside the company. Patricia McBride was the nation's leading ballerina, but within the New York City Ballet she was just one of the principals. Peter Martins won rave reviews for his work, and several of the later Balanchine ballets, Union Jack and Vienna Waltzes, made Martins the equal of a Broadway star, but not in the company.

There was one star with NYCB, and that was dance. There actually was one other star, Balanchine, who created the dance. He was a world figure, the best choreographer of the 20th century. He brought his company to Saratoga in 1966, developed an audience, and became a part of the Saratoga summer scene. Confirmation of this was made on July 15, 1977, when Saratoga declared it was "George Balanchine Day." The Russian dance master rode down Broadway in a horse-drawn carriage as hundreds lined the streets to applaud and cheer. A park in the center of town was named for him and he was a celebrity despite himself.

Many believed this outpouring of affection and admiration changed Balanchine's thinking about developing stars with the company. He let loose of Martins, and the big Scandinavian started getting more personality on the stage, not just dancing the lines written for him by Balanchine. Martins started dancing a part of Union Jack with a cigarette in his mouth, and the crowds loved it. In earlier years that would not have happened.

Balanchine had fled his native Russia in the summer of 1924, seeking freedom of expression for his ballet genius. The dance master was taken in by Sergei Diaghilev with his Ballets Russes in Paris. Balanchine had grown as a choreographer, organized his own ballet company, and then with the help of Lincoln Kirstein founded the New York City Ballet.

There was a similar story to Balanchine's, and it was happening to a dancer many believed was the finest male dancer in the world, Mikhail Baryshnikov. He had fled his native Latvia to escape the Russians and had come to America seeking artistic freedom.

Baryshnikov had gained some measure of fame dancing guest appearances with companies in the United States and had starred in a motion picture, "Turning Point." But many believed the young Latvian wanted only one thing, to dance for Balanchine in the New York City Ballet. Balanchine resisted, knowing the Latvian was a superstar of dance, and that he would not fit the mold of a principal dancer with the New York City Ballet.

Eventually even Balanchine knew he would have to allow Baryshnikov to join the company and dance in the classic Russian/American works Balanchine had created for the company. But Balanchine showed that Baryshnikov would join on the master's terms. He signed the Latvian to a contract that went into effect on July 1, 1978. That meant Baryshnikov would make his long-awaited debut with the company on the stage at Saratoga Performing Arts Center, not at New York's Lincoln Center.

The Saratoga season opened for the dancers, and Baryshnikov spent time in master class and learned he was just another principal dancer in a company filled with fine dancers. Balanchine was steadfast despite howls from the media, biting columns by New York critics, stunned by the fact that the world's best dancer was going to make one of the most important debuts of the 20th century in the country, at Saratoga Springs.

The public, the press, and Baryshnikov became impatient. When would the debut take place? Baryshnikov was not listed in any of the scheduled ballets at Saratoga, but everyone close to the company knew one day Balanchine would tell him, "You dance tonight."

One of the most famous Russian ballets of all time is "Coppelia." Balanchine had danced in it as a youth in Russia, and when he fled the country to the west in 1924, one of the three dancers who came with him was Alexandra Danilova, who had been best known for her dancing in "Coppelia." Balanchine had resisted doing a new version of Coppelia, but finally decided to have Madame Danilova join him and prepare the ballet for Saratoga. It had its world premiere on July 17, 1974 at Saratoga, and had become one of the biggest hits Balanchine had ever done. It featured Patricia McBride and had made a star out of mime/actor/dancer Shaun O'Brien.

Balanchine had decided to bring Coppelia back to the SPAC stage during the 1978 season, and there was speculation he might toss Baryshnikov into this work, because of the Russian connection. It was great theatre, and Balanchine was always a step in front of most with his theatrics.

When the first performance of Coppelia came and went and Baryshnikov did not appear, everyone wondered if Balanchine was not going to use the young Latvian in Saratoga.

There was a Saturday afternoon performance of Coppelia, to be sponsored by McDonalds, the restaurant chain. A few carefully selected critics were called Saturday morning and told, "Be there."

Saturday afternoon shows are mostly for children to learn about ballet, and 4,708 turned out. Ronald McDonald opened the show, talking to the children in the audience about ballet, and the curtain went up 20 minutes behind schedule.

Warm applause greeted Saratoga favorite McBride as she appeared on stage and O'Brien, who had purchased a home in Saratoga, got his usual good welcome as he brought out his most famous character, Dr. Coppelius.

Then, part way through the first act, Baryshnikov burst onto the stage. It was history in the making. "He can fly," we wrote in the review, and indeed he could.

Musicians in the pit stood up to see the first appearance of Baryshnikov on the Saratoga stage and his first moments with the New York City Ballet. The audience broke into applause, the show was stopped cold. Baryshnikov walked to the front of the stage and bowed, the cheering and applause continued for several minutes. It was a moment of history in a town where history is no stranger.

The electricity of the moment inspired the entire troupe, and as the show progressed and Baryshnikov started leaping and flying around the big stage, it seemed like he had found a way to hang suspended during his jumps. In the third act, Baryshnikov performed a series of leaps and jumps that seemed to be higher and last longer than any before, and the audience kept up its cheers like a homecoming football crowd.

At the finish, the crowd stood and cheered for long minutes. The main curtain jammed, and the dancers had to walk around it to come out and accept the ovation. All knew they had seen something very special.

No one knew that better than O'Brien, the veteran member of the company, who had taken the meaty role of Dr. Coppelius and made it his own. Baryshnikov and the other dancers knew as well, but it was O'Brien who saved the day. For, when Baryshnikov had burst forth on the stage, making his long-awaited debut with the Ballet, he had missed his cue and came out several minutes early. There was actually nothing for him to do until his character in the dance was scheduled to arrive.

He landed in front of O'Brien, who said in his best Brooklyn stage whisper, "What the hell are you doing here?" The young Latvian was stunned, he didn't know if he should walk off and return on cue or stand around. "Jump," O'Brien told him, "you can jump better than anyone, jump, damn you, jump."

Baryshnikov flew into the air, the crowd started cheering, O'Brien and McBride continued with the script, and soon Baryshnikov's part rolled along, and he performed flawlessly. The audience never knew.

It was true, he could fly, but his first flight at Saratoga was unscheduled.

☙

39

A GENERALLY NICE VISIT

ò.

It was a pleasant, typically low key, unpretentious weekend cocktail party in the comfortable and friendly confines of the Fitzgerald homestead on the main drag of North Creek, where in passing conversation, someone commented how nice it was the "general" was going to speak at the VFW luncheon.

A reporter's curiosity made me ask, "General, what general, someone from the Air Base?"

"No," the obviously unimpressed person with the information said, "Some general from Washington, Morey, Moreland, something like that."

You take a long draw on the bourbon and branch in your hand and press on: "Not Westmoreland is it?"

"Sounds like it," the North Country native nods and drifts off to talk Hudson River water levels for the upcoming White Water Derby with someone across the room.

General William Westmoreland was only the most controversial and powerful General of the Army of the time back in 1971. A native of a little town, Saxon, South Carolina, he had gone to West Point, had a distinguished career, been superintendent of West Point and then was commander, Military Assistance Command, Vietnam. After being named *Time* Magazine's Man of the Year, he now was only chief of staff of the U.S. Army and the ranking member of the Joint Chiefs of Staff. General Westmoreland was the Colin Powell of the day.

Monday morning I called the public information office of the Pentagon, and some very correct major told me because of security reasons, General Westmoreland's travel plans were not announced until three days out. "But," the major's tone went very unmilitary, "if you are covering this, don't plan much for Friday. Call me Wednesday."

You can be sure the flag wasn't all the way up the Pentagon pole on Wednesday when the major's phone was ringing. "I knew you would call early, you're old Army aren't you?" he asked. Admitting I had spent some time as a company clerk in an infantry unit didn't hurt me with this guy at all.

"The General will depart Andrews at 0700 Friday for a flight to Plattsburgh Air Force Base, go by ground vehicle to the VFW Post headquarters, speak, meet with some dependents of Vietnam POWs, be driven back to the AFB, and return to Andrews late PM Friday," the Major told me in his best Army-ese. He gave me the name of the Colonel traveling with the General, the name and number of the Plattsburgh public information officer, and the name of an old Sergeant/Major who would be along and know more about what was happening than anyone else in the party.

"By the way," my now old friend and Washington contact asked me, "How the hell big is Mineville?"

I fell off the chair. The most sought-after military speaker in the free world, a man with instant access to the President of the United States, a military officer who was personally responsible for most of what happened of a military nature in the most controversial war this nation had ever fought, was coming to Mineville. It wasn't even a village, or a town. Mineville is a hamlet where a lot of hard working, patriotic, middle American-type people who work underground in the Republic Steel Corp. iron mines lived. A blip on a map in the Town of Minerva, Essex County, Upstate/Northern New York.

How had the Veterans of Foreign Wars post in this tiny place convinced a General of the Army to come there and speak? It was because of a letter. A letter written by John S. Mischenko, who had served as commander of VFW Post 5802, Mineville, for five years.

"We have faith in our government and in you," Mischenko wrote to a man who had suffered through grillings by Congress and the wrath of anti-war pickets for years. "Please," the VFW Commander asked, "come visit us."

General Westmoreland was deeply touched. He sent for information on Mineville, on the area, and when he read about the tiny place in Northern New York, his boyhood in Saxon, South Carolina flashed through his mind. "I was reading about my home," he told me as we sat off in a corner of the VFW Post after his talk. "I look around here, I listen to these people, I could be home. Except you all have funny accents," he laughed.

Westmoreland arrived at the sturdy, well-used, freshly scrubbed and painted VFW Post about 10:30 a.m. after his morning flight from Andrews Air Force Base to the big SAC base at Plattsburgh. A flag showing his enormous rank fluttered from the staff car fender, security types in and out of uniform were everywhere, but by the time the day ended, they were having lunch, the buttons in their ears hanging loose. No one in Mineville would think of even raising their voice at a General who was a guest. This was not a speech in New York or Chicago.

More than 400 persons had gathered for the 18th annual Memorial Day luncheon at VFW Post 5802.

The General was in his "greens," with a chest filled with ribbons, medals, parachutist wings, and the most respected decoration of ground fighters, a Combat Infantryman's Badge. He went with one aide for a tour of the Republic Steel mines, going deep into the earth below Mineville. They gave him a piece of iron ore that came from 3,000 feet below the hamlet. When he handed it to the Sergeant/Major he told him, "I want this in my office, on the display table." When you tell an old Army non-com something like that, you know on Monday morning, when the General arrived to face a week of problems around the world, sitting on the table would be the iron ore from Mineville.

The General was introduced to the crowd, who sat at tables in the main room of the Post, and he was warmly welcomed. He spoke for 39 minutes, reading from a 13-page speech, but he departed from the "official" text on several occasions.

"I feel very much at home here," the former commander of all forces fighting in the Vietnam War, told the audience. "I lived in a mill town too, only we had a cotton mill. You sent Joe Stancook to West Point, Saxon sent me. You sent Johnny Podres to the Brooklyn Dodgers, Saxon sent Ernie White to the St. Louis Cardinals."

The General was stunned to learn that Mineville had lost two of its sons in the Korean War, but the tiny place had seen five die in Vietnam. He praised the patriotism of the community, noting it was such places that kept the nation strong and free.

He told of how he was trying to change the U.S. Army. "We want the Army to be more professional," he said, "but discipline is still the backbone of fighting men. Our goal is to be a modern army, not a 'mod' army."

He drew applause when he mentioned how welcome he felt in Mineville and how he appreciated the fact there were no protesters or anti-war pickets. "I know you know and everyone, everywhere should know," he said, "every member of the U.S. Army is an anti-war advocate."

During the ceremonies for Memorial Day, seven-year-old Mark Conklin came to the microphone, a glass of water in hand. Climbing on a chair he asked everyone to toast, "General Westmoreland and my father." There was not a dry eye in the house as the courageous little boy held up his glass.

Mark's dad is U.S. Air Force Major Doug Conklin, who was one of 378 prisoners of war being held in North Vietnam after being shot down in a bombing raid. The boy and his mother were living in military housing on the nearby Plattsburgh Air Force Base.

During his remarks, the General praised the courage of the prisoners and also the families waiting for them at home, making special mention of the Conklins.

As he walked up to the VFW Post, an honor guard of veterans stood at attention as the General passed. He saluted them and walked over to meet the group. "This is the finest veterans honor guard I have ever inspected," he told them, "good job." Men at attention don't usually grin, but these did.

The Moriah High School Band was playing to welcome Westmoreland, and he broke away from the official party to go up to Band Director James Conley. "All soldiers love bands," he said, "and this is a good one. I played in the high school band in Saxon. Where is the flute section? I played flute."

And with that he strode into the heart of the band to talk with the astonished flute players, and his security officers, realizing this was not the usual assignment, just got out of the way.

He made a special effort to meet and talk with all the Gold Star mothers, who wore their gold and white capes. He held the hand of each and talked privately, listening to their stories, admiring the pictures of their sons, who, under his command, had died.

Raymond Wright walked forward to meet the General, who saluted him first, the traditional measure of respect paid by all officers to anyone of any rank wearing the Congressional Medal of Honor. Wright had won the nation's highest honor for valor in action in Vietnam, an award for which Westmoreland had to sign the final papers. They too talked privately, two soldiers with memories of a far-off war.

Four hours after he had arrived, the security people were getting edgy, they weren't used to being in one place for so long, having people all around the General, even though they knew this was a special place.

His aide told the General as firmly as a Colonel can tell the Chief of Staff of the Army, it was time to leave.

Westmoreland mounted the stage one more time. "Thank you all," the tired-looking old soldier told the cheering crowd, "this has been a great day for me."

"And for Mineville, and for America," Post Commander John Mischenko said, saluting, as Westmoreland ducked into his car and was gone.

ह

40

EVERY FAMILY NEEDS A DOG

The oldest boy came home one afternoon from sixth grade and told us: "We are getting a dog. Mr. Chase has some puppies and I can have one of them. I'll take care of him," he lied, "and we really need a dog."

I had grown up with a succession of dogs, but my New York City bred and raised bride knew from nothing about dogs. But an 11-year-old boy and his younger brothers can be convincing, and the next day a puppy came into our lives. Her mother was a pointer, and her father was a traveling man, so Muffin was a mixture of a few breeds, a Great American Mutt.

We got her housebroken, explained to her the dog bed in the kitchen was hers, and told her about the road. One morning I was on the phone from the office to home when the convinced mother exclaimed, "Muffin just got hit by a car." Carried to the lawn by heartbroken kids, taken to the vet by their panicked mother, she had a separated shoulder, and the knowledge we had spoken the truth about the road, which she has avoided since.

That was all 16 years ago, and since then she has become somewhat famous, and a wonderful character. It is true the girls tolerated her, and the boys enjoyed her while they grew up, but individually all would admit it was a mutually good experience.

Muffin went through the teen-age experience with all the kids. She learned to mooch at the table and how to become an absolute pest when kids were sitting on the living room floor watching TV.

She soon became quite well known as "Muffin, the Junk Food Dog" and her exploits of begging potato chips, dip and cheese anythings became a regular feature of my then-weekly newspaper column. Things I could never tell on the kids, I could always tell about Muffin.

Banks started handing out Milk Bones about the time the kids were getting their licenses, and they would go from drive-in teller to drive-in teller getting her a good supply. She would lean out the window of the car as they sent in their checks from some job to be cashed and await the return of the canister more eagerly for the bone than they did for the cash.

Whenever she got into a snit, she would run away, but only to her grandmother's a few blocks away. She would stay a few hours, beg some raw hamburg from the unending supply in the fridge, and soon ride back home with Grandpa Mitch, one of her truest friends. After he died, she couldn't understand why she had to wait for one of the kids to pick her up. During her younger years she used to ride in the police cars, as the patrol officers would see her heading down Crandall Street and would bring her home.

I had my ego put firmly in place one day when I was parked in Bank Square, and Captain Stanley Wood was showing a rookie cop around the Square. I heard him tell the young officer, "There is someone over here I want you to meet." As he walked over, I turned to meet the new cop. Woody nodded hello, leaned into the back seat and told the rookie: "This is Muffin. If you see her wandering down Crandall Street toward her grandmother's, pick her up and bring her home." So much for my importance in town.

Muffin loves Christmas. She likes the tree, opening presents, and the general confusion of the day. She runs from kid to kid to watch paper come off packages, sniff whatever was new, and hope someone would open her new toy or box of snacks.

She is also an ice cream freak. Drive up Route 9 in the summer, and she gets all kinds of nervous as you approach Martha's. She is afraid you might not stop. She hates other people's diets, since they might not want any ice cream and drive by. Muffin always orders a cone, she does not like her ice cream in a dish. She licks the ice cream away, then chews up the cone, bite by bite, before sitting in front of you to make you feel guilty about eating your ice cream.

She had finished her cone one evening, was begging for mine, when a nice old man passed by. "Why don't you get that poor dog some ice cream?," he said. He was back in a couple of minutes with a small dish for her. "Here doggy," he said, "you can have your own ice cream." She overlooked the fact it had come in a dish and ate it anyway, and learned if she looked sad enough people would buy her a second helping.

She went away on vacation with us once, to a rented house in Wilmington, near Whiteface Mountain. We went over to Lake Placid for an afternoon, and a storm blew down a tree on the house while we were gone. She never forgave us and thought vacations were dumb after that.

She does enjoy her summer home on Lake George, where she tries to spend as much time as possible. In her younger days, she chased chipmunks as a sport. She used to chase the ducks too, but one spring day a duck on the end of the dock moved aside, and she sailed on past to take a dip in the still-icy lake. So much for the ducks, she now tolerates them.

We have watched her drinking problem since her episode at the Lake George Club. We were in the old mahogany boat, the one where she sits on top of the motor cover and surveys the lake like she was Captain of the Horicon, when the Skipper says, "Let's duck into the Lake George Club for a nightcap." We left her tied in the boat and were at the bar when this nice but upset woman comes by to ask, "Do you own a little dog who..." Too late, she roars through the dining room and into the bar. What can you do, you've got to buy her a drink, she's there. She puts away a saucer or two of beer, and is ready to tackle the lake again.

The biggest change in her life came when her former master grew up, got married, and got his own dog, a massive Doberman, Olive Oyle. On its first visit they got into an argument about her food dish, which she does not intend to share. Soon, two dishes were out on the kitchen floor, hers and theirs, as another Doberman, Sophie, and then Malcolm, a Brittany Spaniel joined the group of visitors. You may not be able to teach an old dog new tricks, but she has learned to eat their dry dog food, something she turned her nose up at for ten years.

She is now in her final stage. Her hips hurt, she is deaf, and the walk around the Point at the lake is longer than it used to be. She can still jump around when she thinks you are going for a walk, stays behind you on the walk out and ahead of you on the walk back, but she sleeps a lot before and after.

It is tough for her to get into the car now, and she will only ride with her best friend, the New Yorker who learned all about having a dog from her. They are very close and have a great understanding.

She still loves the sun, and each morning at home, after she has barked at the newspaper carrier during her early morning inspection of the lawn, returns to the kitchen and settles down just inside the patio doors to catch some rays. One of the young dogs tried this and found the warming sun to her liking and put her considerable bulk on the only spot of the rug where the sun reached. Enter the old dog to find her favorite place filled with 100 pounds of young Doberman. There was a brief exchange, and the young dog found another location.

During the afternoon, Olive Oyle likes to nap in the bed in one of the kids' former rooms on the first floor. You notice I didn't say "on the bed," but "in the bed." This massive baby is so insecure she has to pull up the covers and get completely underneath, including her head. The old pooch hasn't got an insecure bone in her body, and it took her a while to understand why the bed was always a mess when the big dog was there.

They have come to an understanding on this as well, perhaps Muffin should work at the UN. There is always a part of the covers left undisturbed when the big baby takes her nap. There sleeps the old dog dreaming dreams of chasing chipmunks, mooching ice cream cones, and of growing up the most-loved member of a big family.

ࠅ

41

CHARACTERS

ra

Stories of characters, those unique personalities that are able to do things just a bit differently, seem to focus on persons from the past. There are several reasons for that, primarily because we like to remember those kinds of people with warm feelings, while active characters are often thought of as bores and ill-mannered extroverts.

Glens Falls was filled with characters. Hymie the Tailor was a little guy who fixed your pants, took your bet on a horse, or wrote your number on a policy slip.

There was a woman around town for years who was called Cigar Butt Annie. She would search out bits and pieces of discarded smokes on the street instead of spending her meager cash on fresh cigarettes or cigars. She was a true character, living life by her rules.

Strings Yarter was another special case. Strings was annually sentenced to more time in Warren County jail than there were days in the year. He would get ten days for public intox, serve five or six, get out, and be back that night or the next morning.

Strings made his cash washing police cars at the jail, and pretty much had the run of the place. He would clean up, fish off the sheriff's dock, and if you flipped him a buck for washing your car, slip over to the Delavan for a couple of cold ones.

He loved to direct traffic, and would stumble out of some South Street watering hole, go to the middle of the street on South and Elm streets and direct traffic until some cop told him, "Get in," and it would be up to the "County" for a few days.

Many years ago there was the Blind Indian, a man who would come down from some place on West Mountain, tied to a young fellow by a pole. The old blindman would sell items from a pack basket, and when he had made a few dollars, follow the youngster to a store for groceries, and then go back to his place on the mountain.

Doc Peck was a bit more than a character. He was one of the best amateur magicians in the country. A regular visitor to his place on Glen Street was the great Harry Houdini. They would work on new illusions and magic tricks, which Houdini used on the vaudeville circuit.

Doc Peck lived at 499 Glen, which if you add the numbers comes to 22. Twenty-two is a magic number for magicians. Doc had a pet rooster who could put it away as good as the doctor. They would go into a bar, Doc would belt a few down, and the rooster would drink his beer from a saucer put on the bar. They would both get a nice buzz and then wander out, the rooster on his shoulder.

Doc Cook, who is mentioned at length in this epic, was another of the great characters. He wrote numbers and collected nickels from the parking meters, as well as having been a great star of vaudeville.

So, in the past, this place has had its share of unusual persons, all of which leads me to a story about my friend Joe.

All characters need a good background, something to get them ready to be unique personalities, the sound of a different drummer beating away in their head. Joe had spent many years working for the Disney companies, made a few bucks, and went into the land business to make a lot more.

That brought him to buying and selling, mostly selling, movie theatres. He owned 13 movie houses around here and sold every one of them at least twice, as he kept getting them back as the new owners couldn't sell tickets like he could.

We were discussing his buying and selling of land, businesses, and movie houses one night at the Hilton bar in Vegas, one of his favorite haunts, when he spoke about one of his best land deals.

"I used to own the Aust," he said, "the drive-in theatre in South Glens Falls, and this guy wanted to buy the land around the place. I told him I would sell him the land for $4,000 an acre and the piece was about 140 acres, more or less. This guy tells me, 'none of this more or less stuff, get it surveyed.' So I got it surveyed, cost me $1,500. The survey shows it's 144 acres. I made an extra 16 grand."

Although his home is in Vermont, Joe can more often be found in a suite at the Sands in Las Vegas or a condo in Florida. When the firm that employed me decided to publish a daily newspaper at the international ski show in Vegas, we knew the key to our success would be Joe.

We could get out the best daily any trade show had, but getting a copy outside the room of each of the 10,000 persons registered for the show, by 6 a.m. every day, that's the key.

Joe goes to work at midnight. He leaves the tables, where he has never mastered the success he has in land speculation, and starts having his "guys" drop off bundles of papers at the big hotels. Bellmen bring them around and leave one outside the door of each room that the hotel's computer system tells them has an occupant who is registered for the trade show.

How Joe gets them to do this is the secret. While there is a "charge," like there is for everything in Vegas, that is not what gets the job done. "It's the syrup," Joe smiles.

Everyone who needs or wants something in Las Vegas knows to drop a U.S. Grant into the hand of the bell captain, but Joe wraps the $50s around a quart of U.S. Grade A Vermont maple syrup. He has it FedXed to his suite by the case. "Every year they remember me," he says. "They have been using that syrup, and it's about gone. I'm just in time."

Getting 10,000 newspapers delivered every night in Las Vegas is a relaxing diversion for Joe, especially since he took on his latest form of business, selling and installing bomb detectors in cars.

"Business has been great," he said one night at the Hilton, rolling the snifter in his hands to warm the cognac. "There are people blowing up cars everywhere. You only have to read the *New York Times* to know it's open season on lots of guys, and that makes the bomb detection business real good."

He explained the system he sold is practically foolproof. "This thing is great. We install it so it tests the exhaust pipe, the alternator, the vacuum, the carburetor, anyplace they might put some plastic. For a while there wasn't any way to tell if they rolled it into a ball and tossed it in the exhaust pipe. We lost some customers that way, but you don't have a complaint department in the bomb business. Now it's better, this thing tests the pipe too."

The "thing" he sells is a type of radio transmitter that starts the car. You get away from the car, start it, and let it run for 10 minutes. The heat from the engine or the pipe will blow most bombs inside of 10 minutes. "Chances are," Joe says, "if it hasn't blown up in 10 minutes, it's safe to drive."

Asked if this isn't tough on cars, especially if the bomb goes off, he laughs and says, "But it's kind to the drivers."

Joe said he learned quickly about U.S. foreign policy when he started selling the car bomb detector. "Castro wanted 10 of these things. The State Department jerked me around for six months before I could get there. But then some oil guy in Nigeria wanted some. Since Washington wanted to help Nigeria against OPEC, I was there in three days."

Joe finds local talent to help him when he flies into such nice places as Columbia —"those drug guys are always blowing each other up"— Saudi Arabia —"those oil guys are scared of each other."

His strangest helper was "...a dude I hired in Puerto Rico. We were doing this car and this guy asks me, real serious, 'You need anybody killed?' I told him no, but how much do you get? 'I only charge a $100 cash, but it's got to be somewhere nice, and you got to throw in an airplane ticket and a suite in a good hotel. I love to travel.'"

A few months later, Joe told me he had sold the car bomb detector business. "I got this great offer from a guy in Istanbul. I flew over, delivered 50 units and sold him the whole business. But I have found out this guy doesn't play fair. He sells bombs, too.

"When he gets an order for a bomb, he finds out where it's going, calls them up and sells them a detector for their car. This guy is not nice."

See, even characters play by rules.

&

42

A DIVORCE BY ANY OTHER NAME IS A CHRISTMAS TREE

ಎ

If you believe the leading cause of friction in a marriage is money or jealousy, you have never gone with your spouse to purchase a Christmas tree.

My parents made it through a depression, having polio together (that's when I learned to cook), and other various calamities, but could never agree on a fir tree to stand in our living room for ten days.

My marriage started out the same way. Our first Christmas was three months after we were married. It was nearly a three month marriage. It is amazing what bad taste your partner develops when you cruise around fire company parking lots seeking a green thing for the interior of your house.

And, we only wanted a tiny little tree for a corner of our first apartment. By the next Christmas, we had a house with a huge living room that would need a great tree. We knew our otherwise tranquil marriage would never stand that test.

I was making probably $70 a week. We spent $65 on a fake tree. It was beautiful, and we made it do for decades. Kids were born and brought up with this fancy phony balsam in our living room each holiday. Little kids want the tree up on Thanksgiving and down in mid-January, who cares? Put it up, leave it up. No needles, no fires, just a nice tree that needs dusting every few years, and a can of spray balsam to make it smell good.

Other families would see a partner move out and into a room at the Queensbury after spending a day driving around to select a tree. We smiled, went into the cellar, got the old tree out of its bag and brought it up into the living room. We would let everyone put on all the horrible ornaments they had made in first grade. Then we would hang the ornaments I brought back from journalistic trips to such ornament havens as Austria, Switzerland, and Germany, and we would have a wondrous tree.

The dog would lay on the floor and marvel at the bubble light— we only had one that worked— presents would fill the floor around it, and it would stand majestically until we all got tired of it, and the good twin would take it down.

Every once in a while one of the group would ask, "Tell us the story of the Christmas tree," and I would go on about the tree selection trip I took with my parents when I was about 12. It began as all such trips did, my mom —who like most women of her generation, by her choice, did not drive— would say to my father, "Mitch, we have to go and find a tree." He would make excuses for as long as possible, but he knew the selection of a tree was an inevitable task.

We drove to a service station on Dix Avenue. My father held up a tree and spoke. I know it was Easter before he made another positive statement. My mother lashed out, as only the Irish can do, with comments about his lack of taste, compassion for the family, desire to see the interior of the house look nice, and questions about his family background, if any.

We drove across town to the circus grounds on Broad Street where there were rows and rows of trees standing up, leaning on ropes stretched between posts driven into the ground. Tiny bulbs hung above the trees, causing my mother to comment the bulbs were so few in number and low in wattage to hide the real shapes of the trees. We left.

We drove to Hudson Falls, to another service station. We found many trees that were "too old," "too bushy," "too skinny," and many that were just not it.

The sellers went through a sales program developed by the American Indians to sell trees to the pilgrims —you never heard about the first Christmas, Thanksgiving got all the publicity because of the tree wars— holding up a tree, noting the frozen branches would come down to cover all those bare spots as soon as you, "bring it into the warmth of your house." My mother was not a pilgrim.

We found a place on Route 4 that was a classic Christmas tree sales room. There were the few lightbulbs and a bunch of trees leaning against a rope tied between two long not-working gas pumps. It was a scene from that Jimmy Stewart movie they show six times each Christmas season. They had lots of trees, all with frozen branches that would "come down," but not THE tree.

Time passes, my father is smoking one of his White Owl cigars down to a tiny, very smelly stump. My mother is making non-stop comments about him, the cigar, the French, and me not being much help.

On Upper Glen Street, at Hamburger Haven, which was a golf driving range in the summer, we found her dream tree leaning against the golf shack. We brought it home. My father cut "too much" off the bottom and "not enough" off the top, and it went into the living room.

I thought it looked great, the decorations were in place, the lights gleamed, the gifts were all over the floor, and we were a happy family again. My dad loved his box of cigars, my mother said the new "Evening in Paris" from Boxers would match the bottles on her dresser from last year, and the dog took her rubber bone to bed.

During the night we heard a strange sound. Something like rain in the living room. We found the "wonder tree" had dropped every needle. It was just a bunch of bare branches with lights. My father was told he had been warned the fir was "old, had been cut in August," but he still smiled as he brought it out to the burning barrel in the back yard.

The kids loved to have me tell that story, it picked up one more stop on every telling. They had Grandpa Mitch tell it to them a lot too. My mother would not comment.

So, when our group reached the stage in their life that a fake tree in their living room was not what they wanted, and a live tree was sought for a holiday season, I retired to my office to write a story about the Lake Placid Olympics.

The first year they brought home a live tree, it was so bad we put it in the cellar. We do not have a fancy room in the cellar, only a washer and dryer, six tons of old clothes and ski equipment for the revival of the 10th Mountain Division. That tree was ugly. They agreed, and the old fake stayed in the living room.

Next year, they started early. No fake tree this year, a real tree in the living room, and mom and dad would go get it. We drove out of the yard knowing our long and happy time together was probably to end within the hour. We drove up to Paul Vesterby's lot on West Mountain Road, walked up to a tree, which I held up. "Looks good to me," I said. "Me too," she said. We bought it, brought it home and left it in a bucket of water in the yard.

Some of the kids came home from college early when called by younger siblings to be told we had bought a tree, which we both liked. The Miracle on 34th Street was the Miracle on Coolidge Avenue that year. They all looked, they all agreed. Great tree!

We came home from the big Christmas dance/dinner at the Sagamore and found the little sister and the nice twin had put up and decorated the first real tree our house had ever seen. Its branches had come down from the heat and were laden with decorations made by little hands over the years and all the nice stuff too.

The dog slept where she could see the bubble light, the presents got needles on them, and you had to crawl on your tummy to get water into the stand, but we loved it, and have put a real tree in the window each Christmas since.

I know, one Christmas night, when our children and their children have gone home, we shall hear a sound like rain in the living room. I will sing a little tune: "It isn't raining rain you know, it's raining balsam needles."

æ

43

LET'S GO FOR A SWIM

ટે•

Nearly everyone who has seen it agrees with Thomas Jefferson, Lake George is one of the most beautiful bodies of water in the world. But those things that make it so attractive, the dozens of islands, the mountains that rise right from the water, the twisting 32 miles over rock shelfs and cold springs make it one of the most difficult distance swims available.

Many people had challenged the relatively short long-distance swim from LaChute Creek to the beach at Lake George Village. There was a major contest held in the late 1920s, but no one accomplished the feat until a 25-year-old woman did it in 1958. Two men did it during the 1960s, and another woman conquered the lake in 1977.

Lake George has rested between its two mountain ranges for thousands of years, ever since the last ice age melted back and left it there. Recorded history mentions the lake in the mountains as Andiartarocte, so named by members of the Iroquois Confederation. A Jesuit priest is the first recorded white man to view the water, and St. Isaac Jogues called it Lac de St. Sacrament. The early natives called it by another Indian name, Horicon, and then the British re-named it for their king.

Eons ago, Lake George got its start in what we now call the Narrows, the group of islands above Bolton Landing. The Indians told their French allies to build their boats in Ticonderoga and they would be able to sail them down the lake and into the Hudson River. They never found the route, but it is thought to have been a passageway that began in Dunham's Bay and continued through what is wetlands to a point near the Big Boom on the Hudson.

Water still flows in two directions out of the Narrows, and that is where the swimmers get into trouble.

After the contests of the 1930s, the first major attempt to swim the lake came in 1950. A 17-year-old senior at Scotia High School, Diane Struble, practiced for weeks in Collins Lake near Scotia, and in August 1950 entered the lake in LaChute or Ticonderoga Creek in an attempt to swim to the village.

Eighteen hours later, after having covered a zig zag course of 25 miles, she was less than halfway down the lake. At 2:05 a.m., her mother, Mrs. Amanda Struble, told her exhausted, sick, and disappointed daughter, "Enough, get in the boat," and the Lake had won again.

She would be back. With the help of Paul Lukaris, owner of Animal Land on Route 9 and president of the Lake George Chamber of Commerce, who became her business manager, and the most colorful guy to ever strap on a pair of six guns and the badge that anointed him as sheriff of Warren County, the late Carl McCoy, she trained all during the summer of 1957. She swam from the Village to Bolton and back to build up interest in the swim and endurance in her stroke.

At 10:30 a.m., Friday, August 22, 1958, covered with five pounds of grease, she slipped into the water of LaChute Creek from a rock that now bears her name. Sylvester Kneeshaw of Bolton Landing set her course, got her through the Narrows, fed her hamburgers from a camper's stove in Rogers Rock State Park, and brought her to the village. At 10 p.m. Saturday, August 23, Diane Struble stumbled ashore, as 10,000 persons cheered, the first recorded person to swim the length of Lake George.

There was far less fanfare in September 1962, as a 31-year-old ex-Marine from Little Ferry, New Jersey, William Stevens, set the record for swimming the lake. He covered the distance in 31 hours, 27 minutes, and went blind from sunburn several miles from the village. He followed the sound of his coach's voice the last six miles and spent four days in Glens Falls Hospital recovering.

A powerful and dedicated 17-year-old, George Dempsey of Troy, swimming for the Lansingburgh Boy's Club, trained in the pool at Roaring Brook and beat the lake in August 1967. With his coach and trainer Bill Legacy in the guide boat, Dempsey was well ahead of Steven's record when a storm blew up with the swimmer only nine miles from the finish. Those nine miles took him 11 tough hours, and he missed the record by 48 minutes.

The trip down the lake with Stella Taylor was an epic journey. It was again led by Kneeshaw, and it was his skills and her determination and ability that beat the lake, which used its full bag of tricks to stop the swim.

"The north wind always dies down at sunset," Kneeshaw told the little band accompanying Taylor on the swim. For most of his six decades on Lake George, that was normally always true. The night of Saturday, June 11, and the morning of Sunday, June 12, 1977, it was not. The north wind was cruel, it whipped up the lake, made handling the boats difficult, and swimming nearly impossible.

It started to rain as the group entered the Mother Bunch Islands. As the rain blew across the spotlights from the lead boat, "Escape" diver George Gumuka exclaimed, "It's snowing." We all believed him.

Bill Wilson drove "Escape," setting the course with Kneeshaw and Milt Latham. They carried divers Gumuka of Lake George and George Goodwin of Boston, while her coaches Jackson Roach and Bob Duenkel were in an aluminum rowboat. Our contacts with the outside world were Joe Scully in the Warren County Sheriff's Department patrol boat and the WWSC Newsboat manned by Don and Larry Weaver and myself, broadcasting every 30 minutes to the radio audience that stayed up all night to follow the journey of this dedicated swimmer.

It was a miserable night. Winds, waves, cold, piercing rain, darkness that kept all landmarks hidden away, a sense of being completely alone, bobbing along in a huge tank, no uplifting signs of progress ever visible.

The unrelenting north wind kept pushing Stella Taylor toward the village, but it also kept pounding her back with endless swells of rolling whitecaps. On Friday there was no sun to warm her back and shoulders, and as night took over, the cold became a chill. When she spoke from the water her teeth chattered. The pitching waves made it nearly impossible for her to eat and take the nourishment and warmth that would sustain her on this swim. And, when she did manage to eat, her abused body rejected the needed food.

She wore a favorite blue bathing cap, which made it nearly impossible to see her amidst the rollers in the darkness. A white cap was sent out, passed to the guide boat, where it still was at the end of the swim. There had been no opportunity to change.

Latham held a spotlight on the waves for hours, keeping it away from Stella so it would not blind her, but keeping the area around her illuminated.

The coaches went on ahead, Duenkel waving the light of a red traffic wand so the swimmer could follow the course. He held that light above his head for ten hours, and as daylight finally came, held up his arms to guide her course.

As we passed Floating Battery Island, Stella Taylor's voice came from the darkness. "I've gone as far as I can go, I can't go any farther." Duenkel told her, "OK Stella, swim over here to this boat."

"I can't," she said between sobs, "I'm too cold."

As he rowed away, she screamed from the water, "Mr. Kneeshaw, please get me out."

Sylvester Kneeshaw has heard that cry before from tired, cold, depressed, frightened swimmers. He leaned over from the back of the "Escape" to tell her: "Come on Stella, keep on coming, just a few more strokes, keep on coming." He told her that 1,000 more times in the next 12 hours.

The worst moment, if there could be a worst moment in that nightmare time, came as the tiny fleet passed through the 30-foot channel at 14-Mile Island. The wind blew the "Escape" ahead, the rowboat got away from Stella. Darkness settled over her as the lights moved away, and she swam into a marker. Not knowing what it was, she slapped at it. The bobbing buoy moved away, then came back in her face. She panicked, began to scream and take in water.

Wilson somehow stopped the drifting "Escape," turned the 28-foot boat around in the 30-foot channel, with Gumuka holding off a dock with his feet off the back, and returned to the floundering swimmer.

Everyone was yelling at her, telling her not to worry, there were no sharks in Lake George. Soon the lights showed the terrified swimmer the bobbing marker. We all laughed, even Taylor. As we turned down the lake everyone knew she would make it.

During the early morning hours, Scully drove away and returned to drop off a passenger. Someone remarked, "My God, it's a priest, what's wrong? Welcome aboard, Father, we can use any influence you have with Him."

The Rev. Robert Purcell of St. Alphonsus Church in Glens Falls had not come to still the waters. He had been listening to our broadcasts and realized how awful it was on the lake. He had been on hand to see Stella off at Diane's Rock and had decided it was time to go onto the lake and just offer his reassurance.

As he was transferred back to the patrol boat for a ride to shore he told the coaches, "Tell her I was here. We are all praying for her."

"Don't forget any of us out here in those prayers Father," a voice said, and he was gone into the darkness.

Dawn brought the rising of the moon over Shelving Rock and what had been an angry lake turned into a ferocious inland sea. Waves four and five feet high tossed the "Escape" around like a cork and the rowboat was unmanageable. We pulled our little boat ashore on Long Island to grab hot coffee, gasoline, and dry shirts, but there was no rest for Taylor, who was being tossed around like a rag doll.

Soon crowds were lining the shores. They held up radios to show they were listening. They rang bells at Frontier Village and the Minne-Ha-Ha steamed out blowing its whistle. Don Weaver put it well as he struggled to hold the boat on course with our little band, "Doesn't this get the adrenaline going?"

It did, and a few hours later, thousands cheered as she crawled ashore and then told us because of the cold she had lost the use of her legs at Baldwin, an hour into the swim, but she had finished.

It was a memorable night on a memorable lake. The little band of 12 had become a family, drawn together like men in war. Lake George had given them her best shot, and they had won.

&

44

JUST ONCE MORE—
LAKE GEORGE

ào

Just once more I would like to spend some time in the Lake George Village that I remember, and that I know from the stories that got told in George McGowan's Sky Harbor.

I would like to drop by Slim's Little Place, a real diner that was tucked into a driveway for the Lake George Garage on Canada Street, and see the tall, slender owner behind the counter, in front of the grill. Order a hamburger or some breakfast that came with great conversation, tips on horses, and all the latest news of what was happening and to whom throughout the village.

Just once more let me drive the old vacuum shift Chevrolet patrol car down the Beach Road, park in the Pit and slide onto a stool at Joe Garcia's for lunch.

Ride during the day with Al Whalen, Slim Cruden, or Howard Busch, the old Glens Falls cop who came out of retirement to work summers at Lake George Beach State Park. Hear him tell Glens Falls stories of battles in the Rockwell House or on South Street, and have him quiet a rowdy beach party by holding up one enormous hand. Ride at night with Bob Haber and swap war stories with Jack Streeter, the old Seabee who had real war stories from the Pacific to tell.

Listen to Superintendent Jim Magee talk about the French and Indian War, and what had happened in Fort George Park and over at Fort William Henry, only this time I would realize he was the top authority on that long-ago conflict I would ever meet.

Watch Mike Dolan come slowly up the concrete from the turnstiles, bags of quarters in each big, Irish hand, his soft smile keeping everyone calm on the busiest days a heat-wave summer could throw at us.

Listen to Chet Ross talk about pitching with a left hander named Whitey Ford as they battled in the minor leagues for a spot in the "bigs."

Watch the reaction of some young motorist who just got pulled over, as Deputies Robert Blaise and Robert Lilly took their towering frames out the door of a Warren County vehicle and approached his car.

Just once more I would like to hear the Jive Bombers wail away on "Bad Boy" at the Airport Inn and watch the plane float in the heat above the bar. Visit the Colonel's Table, Spagnas's Cross Trails, or the Canteen with Nick Marzola checking liquor licenses and the crowds.

Just once more can't we visit with Tommy Rossiter at the Orchard House or drop by Usher's and visit with Jim? Listen to Pierre play the accordion at the Garrison and have lunch at the Sailboat Inn?

It was a great place, filled with wonderful characters. Was there ever a mayor like Bob Caldwell? Retired from the railroad, in a town named for his family, he was the uncrowned king. Pistol in his belt, a walking stick and a jaunty word for all, he charmed the out-of-town reporters who poured into his village for the riotous holidays in the 60s. He was more the sheriff of a Louisiana Parish than mayor of an Adirondack village.

Sheriff Carl K. McCoy, with pearl handled six-guns in tooled leather holsters, a well-shaped cowboy hat, colorful uniform, Camel cigarette's Sheriff for America, smiling off the back cover of *Life*, *Look*, and any other successful national magazine.

Just one more time let's stop by Birdie and Dave's for a beer. Birdie Moriarity and Dave Seaman, they knew all about ecumenical efforts long before Vatican II.

See Harry Cohan, looking smart in his uniform, leading a group of the Warren County Sheriff's Mounted Patrol after a busy day at his Canada Street stores, the Lake George Sports Shop and Muratorie's. I have later great memories of Cohan as a member of the New York State Athletic Commission and of attending championship fights in the new Madison Square Garden where he was in charge.

Just once more take a ride on the Ranger, the Roamer, the Patricia, or zoom up toward Bolton aboard the *Miss Lake George* leaving a wake of rolling swells in what is now a five-mile-an-hour zone.

Thankfully you still can play a round of miniature golf at Parrotts on the corner, just as my dad and mom did on dates more than 60 years ago.

But you can't take a new Ford on a test drive from J.R. Earls, or walk through the lobby of the historic Fort William Henry Hotel.

No one needs to ever return to the battles of the 60s, as hundreds of police would arrest a thousand people on a weekend, carting them to Warren County jail on a school bus.

Just once more, let's have a late nite supper or a 5 a.m. breakfast at Phil's, a plate of spaghetti at Vincent's, and a cold brew at the Delevan bar.

Watch Tommy Rossiter run the justice court, and listen to the wisdom of Judges Ralph Brynes and John Dier as they dispensed justice to hundreds of young perps on a busy weekend.

Just once more, let me cover the news in the street with Ed Lewi before we both have to move off to other much less fun things in life that will keep us in touch, but never back together on the news beat.

Let's grab dinner at the Jolly Roger on the Lake, watch a plane taxi up and tie down at Sky Harbor, or go by Joe Seaman's Log Cabin grocery.

Will there ever be trials like the ones in the old courtroom of the County Building? John Hall, Esq., matching wits with J. Clarence Herlihy, as a jury sat behind the polished railings of the old courtroom straining to hear.

Jailer Milfred Pratt tossing Strings Yarter the keys so the jail's most popular prisoner could lock himself in for the night after a day of washing cars, fishing off the dock, and sneaking over to the Delevan for a beer.

It would be nice to stop in the A&P for a three-pound bag of fresh ground Eight O'Clock coffee, go up the street to Louie's Bakery for a blueberry pie, and stop by Foley's to have some steaks cut.

On a rainy day, catch a film at the Lake George Theatre.

Meeting Curt Hughes, then a young priest working at St. Mary's in Glens Falls at the Anchor Camp and picking up your best girl at her folks' cabin at Ben Greene's Snug Harbor are great memories. They both went on to better things, he's a pastor, she's your bride. Well, at least he went on to better things.

Just once more, let us gas up the Shepard from a dock boy working at Hall's with Mr. Hall or Betty always coming out to say hello.

Watch the Lake George village cops work miracles with traffic on the Fourth of July, and Chief Dewey Sims running the Lake George town cops from the tiny office deep off Canada Street.

Play nine holes at Yonder Hill after work, take a shower, and catch up on the news at the bar before going back to the "Falls."

Live all summer in a tent in Battleground Park so you could work two shifts at the "Beach" and have enough cash to go back to school in September. What a crew at the Million Dollar Beach, one's a priest, one was the mayor of Troy, one wrote this book, John Herlihy's an attorney, and Dick Carota is doing just fine running Finch, Pruyn Paper Company, all graduates of Jim Magee's staff.

In 20 years' time, one of my group will write about his time at the Neptune, Charlie's, and the like. I hope he enjoyed it as much as his dad, Hank Eichen, Pete Smith, and their generation did, and hopes he could do it all, "just once more."

ɘ

45

NUNS

❧

Glens Falls was a place blessed with wonderful kindergarten teachers. Starting school in this town was helped by caring teachers who sent worried mothers home and helped little ones grow and mature as well as feel secure in their new world of the classroom.

My beginnings were with Mrs. Lamb, who was a legend at Jackson Heights School. Her morning and afternoon kindergarten classes could serve as clinics on how kids should begin the 13 years they were to spend in education. Just enough challenge to make it interesting, just enough caring to make it secure, just enough freedom to let you grow, and just enough discipline so you could learn to live with others under society's rules.

While I was at Jackson Heights, many of the young people I was to spend most of my school years with were growing under the loving hand of Sister Edwina, another legend in her time, who ran (the operative word here is *ran*) the kindergarten class at St. Mary's Academy.

The other people who were to be my classmates in a few years were getting their start in educational life from Sister Stanislaws (Sister Santa Claus to the little ones) at St. Alphonsus School.

I am sure there were other fine kindergarten teachers in this community at the time and others will have their memories of them, but those three were the teachers who shaped the minds and bodies of the people I was to grow up with as schoolmates. Thankfully my kids had the same great experience as they were exposed to two of the finest kindergarten teachers ever to take on that incredible challenge. One spent some time with Sister Roberta at St. Mary's and all of my group passed through the loving classroom of Mrs. Casey at Kensington Road.

I stayed at Jackson Heights through fourth grade, and then we moved. I wound up in fifth grade at St. Mary's and met a new group of people who would greatly influence my life: nuns. The Sisters of St. Joseph held forth at St. Mary's, and these black-robed women in their starched white bibs and head bands, who seemed to glide, not walk, had eyes on all four sides of their head, and we were sure spoke directly with God each day for instructions, were the unquestioned rulers of our lives from 8:30 a.m. to 3:30 p.m. every day.

There is a very popular play that will be around for a long time, "Nunsense." If you go to see it you will find a lot of the audience laughs when the nuns click their clickers and ask their questions. Watch the ones who sweat, who try not to be seen in their seats, who sit up and look straight ahead. Those are the ones who lived that experience.

I learned very early in the fifth grade at St. Mary's Academy, when a nun says, "Hold out your hand," she is not going to give you candy. And when that ruler comes down on your knuckles, don't flinch. And, if the nun does rap your hand, or does other things to your tiny psyche, don't, under any circumstances, go home and tell your father. He will not take your side in any argument with a Sister of St. Joseph, and will complete the punishment program the "good sister" initiated.

I remember we had a nun who came into our classroom a couple of times a week to teach us music. Sister Ann Maurice was one of the prettiest women I had ever seen. I mentioned this to one of the Irish lads who had been in the Academy since the beginning. "Don't say that," he said turning white and blessing himself over and over, his Irish home training leaping to the fore. "Don't you know you can't say things like that about nuns?"

I kept it to myself after that, but I thought Sister Ann Maurice was beautiful.

Time passed, and I learned the rules. Raise your hand when you want to answer a question, stand up to speak, do your homework, and if you didn't know the answer, don't ever fake it. These women knew everything, or at least we thought they did.

I had some great perks, which I developed to their fullest. My grand-pere was a butcher across the street in the Mohican Market. That discovered, I was the one sent a couple of times a week to pick up meat for the convent. I would go across the street and get the packages, which was always good for a jelly donut from the bakery. "Donnie, are you getting the groceries for the nuns? Well then, here's a donut, enjoy it on the way to the convent."

At the convent, the saintly old nun/cook would find the extras that grand-pere had stuffed into the packages. "God bless you, boy," she would say. "Your grandfather has been kind to us again. Sit down here, I just made cookies." Now there was a nice way to kill half an hour twice a week when you were 12.

Then came the eighth grade. The nun mistakenly assigned to that tough grade and age group did not like teen-age boys. Glens Falls High School built one of its finest teams in history from young athletes she drove from the halls of St. Mary's to Glens Falls Junior High School. This had been going on a few years when I got into that classroom. I never had many problems with the sisters, but with her I hit a wall. One Friday afternoon in mid-September I took all my books, in Catholic school you own the books or at least you did then, went to church as we all did each Friday, and when I got home informed my unbelieving parents I had spent my very last day in that classroom.

A couple of phone calls and at 8:30 a.m. Monday I was the newest pupil in the eighth grade at St. Alphonsus School. It was one of the great moves of my life. The "French nuns" were the same, but different, and that year was one of the best ever spent. It started on a terrible note. "Mr. Metivier," the nun said using the French pronunciation I had only heard from grand-pere before, "What is an adverb?"

"Well," I stammered, "an adverb is a word that replaces a verb." The class laughed, the nun commented, "and they told me you want to be a writer. We have work to do," and we spent a wonderful year doing it.

Four years of high school back at the Academy brought forth some great relationships with some bright, interesting, and challenging teachers. Sister James (Jimmie) knew an adverb didn't replace a verb, and about all the writers who used them. Sister Aldred (Ally Oop) who put the football captain into a five-inch wide locker—and shut the door. Sister Patrick Frances who could even teach boys how to touch type. Sister Catherine Bede, the intellectual who proved Latin was anything but a dead language.

Then poor Sister Gertrude Joseph, who spent more than two years of her life trying to get a dumb French kid from the west side to understand geometry. The first regents, 15. "They gave you 10 points for your name on the blue book," she said, starting over. The second regents, 50. "Well, if we add the two scores together, you just pass," she smiled. Third time, 69. "You have your math to graduate," she said, "but keep up on your writing."

Perhaps the best thing they taught us was order. The up stairs were used for going up, the down strairs for coming down. Late for a class, you still use the correct stairs, even if they were empty. Hot today?, tough, keep your tie up around your neck. Discouraged, upset?, offer it up for the "poor souls."

Find something very difficult, try harder, but don't quit. When you left St. Mary's, you had a diploma worth something and self-discipline to see you through life. I remember an old Army drill sergeant in basic training who growled at me one cold December morning, "You must have gone to school with the sisters." I was proud of that.

Not only are they all gone now, St. Mary's Academy ends at the eighth grade, and St. Alphonsus School is part of it. The Sisters of St. Joseph and the French nuns are memories. When I wrote a book several years ago, I sent a copy to a nun still living in the retirement home in Albany. She called. "Great effort," she said. "Do you have a blackboard in your office, good. Write this word on it 50 times, it was misspelled. And, hold out your hand," she laughed.

❧

46

SAILING, SAILING

ಶಿ

If I had been part of the crew, Columbus would be known for discovering the Canary Islands, because that's about as far as we would have sailed.

I like to sail, I even own a sailboat. The Calliope is a wonderful old, five-ton, 27-foot O'Day Outlaw that I bought from my doctor, and if you don't believe me I have the prescription blank bill-of-sale to prove it.

I had been looking for some kind of summer sport to get interested in, now that I am well past my prime for getting 17 friends and choosing up sides for a game of rounders. I ruled out most without getting off the chaise on the porch at the lake house. I thought, very briefly, about running. No way. Those people die. Even the guy who got everyone else up and running died.

A friend of mine is a rock climber, nationally known, has ascents named for him. He hangs on a tiny rope twice a week. He has no skin on his fingers or shins, blisters on his toes, and lots of his body is always sore. He fell a summer ago, and got saved by a rope the size of a clothesline. He did giant swings half a mile above the ground for 20 minutes. His invitations to climb rocks are an easy no.

The kids used to ask me to water ski with them, but now they can't get enough boat time themselves. Besides, the gas bill for the Cobalt already resembles a federal grant to an emerging Central American country. I'll keep my skiing confined to snow.

It is a shame to waste the scenery and the water up here on Lake George, so the decision a few years ago was to try sailing.

We were at the annual auction the Chapman Museum holds to raise needed dollars, and my bride bid and purchased lessons at what was then Patty and Bud Foulke's Lake George Sailing School. During the hottest two weeks of the summer, I ventured out on the lake in a Rainbow, one of the sailing world's great teaching boats, and found Bud Foulke to be a great instructor.

I also spent time in the classroom learning the physics of sailing. No, that is not true. I was in a classroom where the physics of sailing were taught. I did not learn a thing. I took physics in high school for nearly a week. The kindly nun who taught the course took me aside, and said, "Sell your book to someone on the waiting list, go study verbs and nouns, but please leave my physics class, or you will ruin the marking curve."

When Bud Foulke lectured on wind and its reaction to the mass of the sail and the force of the boat slipping through the water, he was not talking my language.

I tried to learn about the knots, the lines, the painters, the sheets, and all the other terms that let you talk "sail-ese" to others of the sailing persuasion. I do remember telltales are the strings you want to keep straight out to show you are catching wind correctly, that you should keep your head down when the boom swings around, and for some strange reason caught on right away to reading wind coming across water. I don't know what to do when it gets there but I know when it's coming.

I tried so hard to learn the terms like "tacking," which is really another word for work, "ready about," "hard-a-lee," and "prepare to jibe." They are easy, except I don't know what to do after I have said them.

So much for becoming a good sailor, but I did enjoy the feeling of running with the wind, of listening to the boat cut through the water without hearing the roar of a motor. Sailing is great fun, and Lake George is a perfect lake on which to sail.

So, when Dr. Bill Tedesco told me he was getting a newer, bigger, faster boat, and the Outlaw was available, I became a captain. My boys worked hard on making the old boat look new again. They sanded, polished, painted, even put in four new windows. The Calliope is a show piece. When we brought her home to the mooring in front of our cottage I did what every owner does, I searched for the perfect name. I wanted to call her "Terpiscor," after the Greek muse of dance, that got voted down. How about "Calliope?" the Greek muse of epic writers, I asked from my keyboard where I was writing a story that would buy that week's groceries. They didn't dare vote no.

Calliope floats at her mooring, a giant wind direction indicator. Her teak shines like the day it came out of Henderson's Boat Yard across the way in Cleverdale years ago. The hull gleams, the huge computer-generated letters shout out her name, and she rides easy on a deep anchor bathed in a spotlight at night. so I can see her from the windows of the room where I write.

The entire scenario is perfect, until I want to take her somewhere. I still don't comprehend the coefficient of friction of the water on the hull, or "hard-a-lee," from whoa. The answer, find a skipper, someone who can turn a boat both ways, knows tack from jibe, sheet from painter, likes to sail on Lake George, and is willing to have a captain who knows only enough about sailing to stay out of the way.

Just my luck, H. John Hendley, Esq., Skipper of the Calliope, is not just a good sailor, but part of a national Rainbow championship crew, and a purist who thinks the motor on this big old boat is a decoration, We have to sail away from the mooring and sail back to the mark if the wind is a wisp of a breeze or a gale. Worse, the rest of our regular crew has the same level of sailing skills I possess.

One September afternoon we were flying across Harris Bay, heeling over with water coming above the rail, fighting a wind that would have made John Paul Jones give up his ship, when I realized, if the Skipper ever fell overboard, we all die. The rest of us would sit there and get blown to Ticonderoga or Fort Edward, and there is no water route to Fort Edward.

So, the crew made a decision to try and learn to help sail that old boat. The Skipper insists we do everything "smartly." So naturally he ends up calling me Don Dumbly because despite his best efforts, it is obvious the Captain and the crew are not America's Cup material.

We shot the mooring one blustery day, he gave me the thing you steer with, the stick in the back, and said, "Hold it on the course for the mark." He went forward and caught the mooring, grabbing the big line from the water as we shot by. "Strike the main," he yelled, and we all looked at him as he tried to hold five tons of boat in a big blow. When we saw his arm start to stretch and thought he might fly over the side, we realized he meant take down the big sail, which we did, but not really smartly.

We have taken that great old boat lots of places. The Skipper can sail it into the wind, on reaches, running (I use those terms because they are written on the sailing watch my group gave me for Father's Day, but I don't know what they mean) all over the lake.

We sail back and forth, he calls it something else, tacking or some such, up Harris Bay, go outside Long Island into the main lake and catch hurricanes looking for the trade routes. We have gone around Long Island, and one rainy Sunday actually sailed it through the tiny gut between Speaker Heck Island at the tip of Assembly Point, no mean feat especially when a Park Commission patrol boat got in our way looking for some kind of sticker or registration. I just was my usual Don Dumbly, and the Skipper talked nautical.

But I do have a summer sport. I don't do much except move out of the way when they bring the sail from one side to the other; there is a name for that maneuver, but it's not written on my watch.

The old boat is fast. Some folks in a boat with a taller mast and lots more sail challenged us one Sunday. We ran away and hid, the old boat flew. It was great fun. So, I asked the Skipper. "When are we going to be ready to race this old boat?"

He bit down hard on the stub of his cherished cigar, lifted his Absolut Citron from the seat, held the glass into the wind, looked us in the eye and muttered, "Never. Ready about...smartly."

a

47

WHAT TO EAT?

ॐ

It finally happened! During a news report, on National Public Radio —where else?— when the announcers were describing how the people, and especially the children, of some previously unheard of place in the world were starving, they interviewed some modern nutritionist who warned we must be careful what we send these unfed unfortunates.

She noted there are so many foodstuffs that are filled with additives, unhealthy colors, too much sodium, nitrates and chicken lips, that we must be sure only to send "healthy foods" to these poor folk.

Can you believe that? Poor Agmar has walked 60 miles across a waterless dessert, and when he arrives at the UN food station all they have are nitrate-filled, sodium-packed hot dogs made with bad parts of chicken with the look of Yellow No. 2. "No, no bloated-belly children," he says, "none of this unhealthy food, we shall walk on to the natural food feeding station in Abudabe."

Now I am all for eating healthy, but the good people at the FDA, OSHA, AMA, FBI, CIA, and National Public Radio have gone too far. The list of things we must not eat because they will cause us to expire has gone past good sense and reached nonsense.

Hot dogs are a good example. This all-American food, which we stole from the Germans and their wursts, is getting a lot of bad press. The good food fairy is warning not to let your little angels eat these processed links filled with bad animal body parts. Forget what sweepings the Germans put in the wurst you eat at the bottom of every decent ski slope in Europe, American hot dogs have been made from the leftovers in slaughterhouses for more decades than any nutritionist has been around to write about how bad they are.

Who would grind a pound of sirloin and stuff it in a tube? The packing houses put some cheap pork, cuts of beef you should not really know about, and in recent times chicken, into a bit of skin, pucker the ends and a tube steak is born.

I remember in the H.C. Metivier Meat Market, hot dogs were connected. Now they come in a package, neatly wrapped, safe from the hands of the butcher. My grand-pere used to pick up a string of hot dogs, look to see who the customer was and knowing how many sat at her dinner table each night, give her enough for all, wrapping them in brownish/orange meat paper and writing the price on the side of the package before he went to slice her some bologna —now also a sodium-nitrate threat.

If you don't go to some high-priced "natural" store, you now can't buy franks by the number, only the package. If you have five people to feed and need 10 hotdogs, the decision of the day is to buy one package and be two short, or buy two packages and have six left over. We never had that problem because at our house a leftover was only peas or broccoli.

There are also those who are preaching coffee is not good for us, and have tried to frighten us with stories of coffee nerves, caffeine addiction, and other health and mental problems blamed on the beverage that keeps this nation's trucks, buses, and navy operating.

Having dinner one evening at the Shoreline in Lake George, Leona Hogarth came over from her piano to talk between sets. The waitress came by with coffee and asked her if she wanted "decaf." Leona noted that she drank "real coffee," and to bring some forthwith, the stronger the better. Since Leona was 93 at the time, I am happy to know whatever coffee does to you takes at least nine decades to work. I am safe.

Not only the liberal nutritionists on NPR preach food safety, I have a member of my group, who spent years scarfing down bowls of puffed sugar for breakfast and bags of sawdust fast food burgers for lunch, who has seen the light. This former junior high school pudge now runs to Warrensburg and back, or bikes around Lake George before his dinner of tofu, raisins, and veggie dogs.

He has tried to convince me the pleasant task of carving up an oversize prime rib for an evening meal is life threatening. I grew up eating handfuls of raw hamburg out of the case at the market, and my late mother kept herself alive a few extra years by eating a half pound of raw, ground sirloin a few times a week. Now I don't recommend this, because I do recognize beef out of today's cases does not resemble the pure, red meat my grand-pere had piled in 20-pound mounds on clean white trays.

Most of the athletes I spent much of my early life around trained on thick steaks. "Wrong, wrong, wrong," my young nutritionist-runner-biker tells me. He explains a theory that the food given to beef cattle to fatten them up, they don't fully digest, and it makes it difficult for you to digest the beef. "It takes four days to digest beef," he claims. "Rice cakes, on the other hand..."

I note Babe Ruth hit 60 home runs living on hot dogs, cheap beer and friendly female fans. "He would have hit 80 on tuna fish sandwiches with whole grain bread," he says.

While our entire way of eating has changed in the past two decades, there are those who have not caught up. If you go through life, especially in a big city, without kids around and are more or less into yourself, you don't know what's happened out there.

I was riding across the Idaho Badlands with a car filled with three newspaper guys and a magazine editor. The editor lived and worked in New York City and was somewhat insulated from America above the Harlem River. In our conversation, we found this sophisticated, cosmopolitan person who had traveled most of the world, had never eaten in a fast-food restaurant.

We decided to end that cultural deprivation by finding Twin Falls' McDonald's. Her entry into the world of Big Macs and their world-famed ingredients ("two all-beef patties, special sauce, lettuce, cheese, pickles, onions on a sesame seed bun") Quarter Pounders, four kinds and three sizes of soda, and two of French fries, was traumatic.

She stood and read the myriad charts listing the food available and asked the startled counter girl for "a medium-cooked hamburger." Everyone in the Twin Falls, Idaho, McDonald's stared, knowing here was a person definitely out of the American mainstream.

An assistant manager, probably specially trained for such occurrences, moved the clerk aside and took this city dweller's first-ever fast-food order. "A medium hamburger, some French fried potatoes and a small soft drink, very little ice." He smiled the smile you give to those you pity, and asked a question he probably remembers to this day. "Anything else?"

"Yes," she said in a firm voice, "can I have a drink of water?"

Silence fell over the fast food emporium. The manager came from the back. He told her there were problems to overcome, cups were used for inventory, there was no way to use one for...stammer...water.

So here we are, having reached a point of being warned to check the nutritional value of the food we give to starving people. But there is hope. Just recently a friend of one of my kids told me he had just seen "something new" at the supermarket. "There is this meat counter and the meat is not wrapped up," he said. "It is sitting out on trays and a guy in a white apron takes your order and cuts you steaks, grinds up meat for hamburg, this is really a great idea," the teen-ager gushed.

Somewhere in butcher heaven I heard my old grand pere chuckle.

❧

48

YOU CAN DO IT NOW

ᘓ

"Where but Glens Falls," the frequent visitor from his August seat in the press box at Saratoga to Hometown U.S.A. asked, "would you go for a hot dog and a shirt?"

He has a point. While the Glens Falls/Saratoga/Adirondack/ Lake George/Bolton Landing/Lake Placid region has a great past, there are lots of people/places/happenings that should be visited today to make memories for tomorrow.

While the Halfway House is gone, and Fan and Bill's is no more, the Wishing Well has moved in nicely to be today's place to be after the races, after you leave Siro's.

The remark about Glens Falls has great significance. Many people who grew up in Glens Falls and had the ill fortune to have to leave, make it a point to visit the New Way Lunch "John the Hots" on South Street for a hot dog or two on any trip home. They have been serving hot dogs with the secret sauce at the New Way since Babe Ruth was hitting home runs for the New York Yankees.

Any attempt to change the hot dog emporium is met with loud cries from the faithful who are still trying to adjust to a new front door. The dogs are cooked on the grill in the window, the rolls are in an old stainless steel steamer, and the heavy white plates have been in use for decades.

While visitors always find their way to the New Way, regulars fill the place most of the time. As I walk through the new front door, a counterman will tell the person working the grill, "Three on one, no onions," and holler to the counter person at the cooler door, "diet with a glass." It is nice to be welcome somewhere.

The New Way Lunch is one of the last remaining memories of Glens Falls' past. It is comfortable, resists change for marketing reasons, and still serves hot dogs and great pie with conversation, as a diner should.

The horseracing writer from Saratoga also made mention of getting a "shirt" in Glens Falls, and he was talking about the Troy Shirtmakers retail store in the Troy building at Lawrence and Cooper Sts. They have been making shirts in that massive old brick structure for generations, and it is still one of the best locations to purchase a 100-percent cotton shirt in the nation.

If you wander into a Neiman-Marcus store in Dallas, a hotel store in trendy Atlanta, or an exclusive Chicago men's shop looking for a private label, cotton men's shirt, chances are it was made and that exclusive label sewn in at Troy Shirt.

Several years ago, Governor Mario Cuomo was standing on a platform in the parking lot of what was the temporary building on Lawrence Street for CB Sports, newly stolen by New York State from Bennington, Vermont. The Governor was there to inspect the CB manufacturing operation and announce the state loans granted to bring in the ski clothing business to New York. Some people in a window of the factory across the street yelled hello to New York State's articulate governor, and he waved back, mentioning to an aide, "Isn't that the shirt place?" Assured it was, after he had won the crowd over with one of his masterful speaking performances, the Governor shook several hundred hands and headed for his limo. He detoured, however, and went to the Troy retail store to stock up on a dozen new shirts.

The area still has many places that deserve a visit to tuck away memories of a kinder, gentler time. Pete Smith runs his East Cove restaurant in a manner that keeps his steady stream of locals happy year round and keeps the tourists standing in line for tables all summer. George Patrick just up Route 9L on the East Side of Lake George has the same happy facility to mix local and tourist business, and not only has well-presented plates of excellent food, but a bar that turns out some of the best mixed drinks in the Lake George area. The village can be hurting from the weather, but the "Cove" and "George's" are usually full, and worth the wait. Three cheers for George, by the way, who once a year fills the former Airport Inn and donates the entire night's proceeds to the Warren County Unit of the American Cancer Society.

Sky Harbor, Birdie and Dave's, Vincent's, and Phil's are gone from the village, but Jim Quirk has built a small empire along the lake back of the Canada Street main stream. The Shoreline kitchens can turn out a fine meal, and if the weather is good, you can eat dinner on the new Horicon and sail the lake.

The Lake George Steamboat Company has been moving people and mail on the lake for more than a century and now have the largest boat on the lake, the Lac du Ste. Sacrament, another place to sail and dine.

Ask anyone from Muffin, our old junk food dog, to the occupants of the chauffeured limos that drive up from polo matches at Saratoga, where's the best soft ice cream in the world?, and the answer is Martha's on the Lake George Road. There is always someone you know standing in one of the lines, and on nights when coffee-flavored Dandee Cream is the feature, go early.

Saratoga is filled with great places, Sperry's for food, the Metro for music, the springs still bubble from the ground, and if you ignore the reports of the do-gooders who say the springs are filled with radium and other glow-in-the-dark problems, you can drink from the same waters the Indians used hundreds of years ago, and Diamond Jim Brady brought his ladies to after a long night on the town.

Not many places have the New York City Opera, the National Dance Museum, the New York City Ballet, the National Museum of Racing, the Philadelphia Orchestra, Saratoga Raceway, and the world's finest thoroughbred track within its confines, so how can you not enjoy Saratoga?

There is always breakfast at the track, lunch on the porch at the Reading Room if you can get a member to invite you, and dinner at a vast choice of fine spots— the Fire House, the Gideon Putnam dining room, Eartha's Kitchen— scores of places around Saratoga Lake, and a dozen on Broadway.

The Spa has some unique places, Hattie's Chicken Shack and Bruno's for wood-fired pizza.

A favorite with the beer-burger-pizza crowd is the authentic Irish Pub, the Parting Glass on Lake Avenue. Your liver may not last to let you sample the more than 100 beers, 20 on tap including Bass ale and Sam Adams Boston lager, but you can go down trying.

Back up north, those in the know go to Massie's for home-made spaghetti and sausage sauce, the Corner Grill for the nation's best club sandwich, Chez Pierre for French, Poopie's for a classic Poopieburger and home fries, Joseph's for a massive buffet lunch, the Blacksmith for steak, the Montcalm for a gracious dinner, and Rathbun's in the hills of Washington County for pancakes with maple syrup that's right out of the trees on the lawns.

Need to impress some snooty New Yorker who thinks he's in the sticks up here? Take him to dinner in the Trillium at the Sagamore, and let him buy the wine.

Need a gift? The Indian Teepee in Bolton Landing has it. Stop for a hot dog at Frank's while you're there, and if it's summer, see if the library is holding its book sale.

The Glens Falls City Band still plays old-fashioned band concerts on Tuesday at Lake George, Wednesday in Warrensburg and on Thursday evenings all summer from the bandstand in Glens Falls City Park.

Lake Placid is a hidden-away treasure with good restaurants, ski jumping in the summer, the Olympic Arena filled with shows, and the nation's best promoter, Ned Harkness, running the Olympic Regional Development Authority, making it all work. You may stop at the Elm Tree in Keene for lunch and a look at the bobsled photos, or in the winter get to ride down the course at Mt. VanHoevenburg. It is, as they claim, "the champagne of thrills."

We may yearn for the return of Donnie Howard and Pat Marino entertaining at the Rustic Inn, and for the Derby Bakery man to ring his bell and provide a package of real jelly donuts, with a swipe of white frosting on top, but we can still find wherever Freddie Blood is playing drums and be sure to enjoy the music. The jelly donuts, though, too bad, they're gone.

&

49

THE CLUB

&

It almost died of neglect, it survived strange rules and a frustrated former employee who tried over and over again to burn it down, but now, the Lake Placid Club, a rambling collection of turn-of-the-century buildings on the shores of Mirror Lake is once again fighting for its life.

The Lake Placid Club has more space devoted to public sitting rooms and endless corridors than to functional meeting and sleeping rooms, but that's the way they built places for ladies and gentlemen in 1895.

As it approaches its centennial, the building that hosted two Winter Olympic Games faces a bleak future, but it has a glorious past.

The massive old resort is a functional designer's nightmare. One could live there six months and still forget how to get to his room. Stairs go off to long halls, which open onto sun porches that overlook some of the most beautiful scenery Lake Placid and the High Peaks of the Adirondacks have to offer.

A step through the stone entrance into the massive lobby is a step back into the Adirondack past. For decades, if you had been a guest there before, chances were the desk clerk would remember you by name. Later, when you walked into the Forest Dining Room, which seated 475, or the Sentinel Dining Room, which held more than 500, they would remember if you liked a window seat or a quiet corner to sip your coffee and read.

The Agora auditorium, complete with theatre seating, has a tremendous fireplace along its left front side and a pipe organ on the opposite wall.

The Forest Library held more than 12,000 books, many of them valuable reference works on Lake Placid, the Adirondacks, and the story of the 1932 Winter Olympic Games.

The Lake Placid Club opened as a cottage in 1895, after Melvil Dewey discovered Lake Placid was a place where he could escape the ravages of his hayfever. Dewey, creator of the famous library classification system, had been searching the United States for a place where he could relax, write, and not be bothered by sneezing and a constantly runny nose.

Dewey and his wife, Annie Godfrey Dewey, originator of the American Home Economics Association, traveled by canoe and then buckboard to reach the Lake Placid area. He found it perfect for his health problem, and the clear, clean air helped her with her problem of rose cold.

Together they founded the Lake Placid Club, and Dewey's stern rules governed who would be, and more importantly to him, who would not be, members.

During the winter of 1904-05, winter sports were introduced; sliding on the ice of Mirror Lake, sleigh rides, and winter hikes, and this attracted many new members, each of whom had to gain the approval of Dewey and his personal rules of what kind of person could belong.

The high standards, the social benefits, and the recreation available attracted many members of wealthy families who in the past had sailed to Europe for winter vacations in the best resorts of the Alps.

The growth curve of the Lake Placid Club was amazing. In 1895 the club had an estate of five acres, and a balance sheet of $10,000. In 1930 it owned 10,000 acres, and its balance sheet was in excess of $4 million.

Dewey insisted the club remain restrictive and exclusive, and his rules would today be in every court in the North Country, but then the restrictions helped it grow and gain in wealth and exclusive membership.

Dewey told friends the Club was to give men breathing time in surroundings of haunting loveliness. "I want it to give them a chance to cleanse themselves, to see things squarely, and think high thoughts."

The highest essential for membership was good character. No matter how prominent or able or wealthy a family might be, if they did not possess that passport to good society which is easier to recognize than define, they were turned away. You could not buy your way into the Lake Placid Club.

Dewey flatly stated: "No one will be received as a member or as a guest against whom there is a physical, moral, social or race objection. This invariable rule is rigidly enforced." And indeed, without benefit of today's civil rights laws and changed social mores, it was.

The founder believed that cigarette smoking should be used in the same manner as the plumbing, out of sight, segregated by sexes, isolated, and well-ventilated.

Dewey banned the use of alcohol, and guests and members used to smuggle liquor into their rooms. In the spring, when the snows melted, bottles would be found littering the lawns where guests had tossed them out of windows high above during the winter months.

The Club gained its greatest fame in hosting the officials for the 1932 Winter Olympic Games. The Games were to play a role in bringing the club back to life nearly 50 years later.

When Lake Placid gained the 1980 Winter Games, it was decided the Lake Placid Club would play host to the International Olympic Committee and the Olympic Committees of the various nations in the Games. The Lake Placid Company obtained loans of $3.5 million to get the ancient buildings ready to host the world. Aided by the infusion of the badly needed capital, the Club came back into the mainstream of great American resorts. Improvements such as 15,000 yards of new carpet, modern plumbing, new wiring, and the like, ate the money quickly.

As the Club prepared to be the focal point of the Winter Games, a disgruntled former employee started a campaign to burn it down. Nearly every night for weeks, a fire was started somewhere in the rambling old building. Finally the Lake Placid Fire Company left trucks on the property, volunteer firemen slept in rooms and scores of New York State Police, aided by federal officers, scoured the grounds to catch the firebug.

The press was moving into the area for the Games and across the lake, in Elan House, home for the Yugoslav-based Elan Ski Company and *Ski Racing Magazine*, we moved into an upstairs back room so photographer Monty Calvert could place a row of cameras facing the Club each night. When the fire siren sounded, he would jump from bed and start to focus in on the old club across Mirror Lake waiting for the flames to shoot into the night sky.

Police caught the firebug before the old Club was destroyed, and it soon was filled with international Olympic officials. It became the social place for the Winter Games and by chance was the site of some of the best celebrations of the 1980 Winter Olympics.

The International Olympic Committee held its annual meeting there during the Games, and for a few days it was the focal point of the major story of the day, because the President of the United States selected that time to announce there would be a boycott of the 1980 Summer Olympic Games in Moscow. So instead of announcing new rules for the lengths of jumping skis or calibres of rifles for the biathlon, the Olympic Committee was facing a major international crisis.

Most of the members of the IOC do not come to the Olympics to spend days and nights working on major problems. They get themselves named to such committees so they can have a nice room, good food, great seats, and attend the best parties at the Olympic Games. In between, they determine where they will go in another four years.

The parties at the Lake Placid Club were famous. One of the Game's major sponsors, Coca Cola, had taken over the Club's boat house on Mirror Lake. They had a non-ending supply of Coke and lots of things that went into it, or into branch water if you wished. Coca Cola has been a major part of every Olympics for decades, and one of the reasons is they know how to keep the people who vote on such things well entertained. The Coca Cola Olympic bash at the Club ensured that the Coke symbol would be in Calgary, Los Angeles, and any other place where the Olympic flag got run up the pole.

One of the great parties at the Club was one hosted by the Crown Prince of Norway. The Norwegians were hosting the World Nordic Championships, always had an alpine World Cup or two each season, and were after a Winter Olympics for a tiny place called Lillehammer, which reportedly made Lake Placid seem a metropolis.

The Crown Prince and his group flew over mountains of salmon, gallons of the schnappes the Norwegians dare the rest of the world to drink with them, and organized a memorable party in the Club.

As luck would have it, the bash was held on the evening the United States hockey team rose up and turned back the Russian Bear on the ice of the Olympic Arena across Mirror Lake. The few Americans at the party had an especially good time celebrating when the final score was announced, and it was made known that the young American skaters had scored the hockey upset of the century.

While the big party of the evening was being hosted by the Norwegians, the Americans and the Canadians took over and gave a clinic on how to celebrate. The IOC guys all got an "A" in the course, and by morning there were still people singing "God Bless America" in a variety of languages, but the booze had run out, and Coca Cola had moved in cases of its product just to keep international whistles wet.

That party and celebration might have been the last of the great nights for the Lake Placid Club. It would not have been a great night for Melvil Dewey, but it was for all those fortunate enough to be there.

The Club held on for a few more years, then was closed to undergo modernization that never happened. Now it awaits its fate, a building out of step with modern demands for heating and cooling and more saleable rooms than public space.

All of us fortunate enough to have spent some time there, to have been involved in any part of its life know that all of its history is not in the Forest Library.

ﬆ

50

ADIRONDACK BIGFOOT

٦٨

"Bigfoot." Just the term envisions a huge, ape-like figure living in the wilds of a forest or in the snow of a high peak mountain. There are reports from veteran Conservation officers that two such characters are living deep in the wilderness of the Adirondacks, the identity of one of them known to some. Both are believed to be persons who made the decision to leave modern-day life and go live in the mountains, as 20th-century hermits.

Stories of other Bigfoot characters abound. There was supposedly one in the mountains at Whitehall, another in the Catskills, and the most famous of all, the Bigfoot creature in the Himalayan Mountains.

While many of the Bigfoot stories are rumor, and others tall tales spun by local woodsmen for visitors, the so-called Adirondack Bigfoot of 1932 was indeed real, and his tragic story very true.

There are actually two versions of the tracking and capture of the Adirondack Bigfoot. One was written by the District Attorney of Essex County, Thomas W. McDonald on April 8, 1932. The other was compiled by this writer through interviews during the summer of 1976 with persons who had been involved in the shooting deep in the woods near Newcomb, most of whom said it was the first time they had talked openly about what happened when a hastily organized posse went into the woods to capture the Adirondack wild man.

There had been stories about an Adirondack Bigfoot, a wild man who had reverted to nature and gone deep into the Adirondacks to live off the land. The "creature" had been spotted a few times and was described as being a huge, hairy man with a footprint nearly a yard across.

New York State Police Sgt. Walter E. Dixon, had retired when he talked with us in August 1976. Sgt. Dixon had been stationed for many years with Troop B in the Adirondacks. He remembered several calls had been received by the State Police concerning a huge, hairy creature. The wild man was blamed for burning down several lumber camps and hunting cabins deep in the woods of Hamilton County.

While State Police knew of the existence of such a wild man, there had been no organized effort to catch him until a night in late February, 1932.

Two cousins, Dick Farrell and Reg Springs of Blue Mountain Lake were trapping in the area of O'Neil Flow on Finch, Pruyn and Co. Inc. property about two miles south of Blue Mountain Lake in Hamilton County.

The two trappers had found a cabin near O'Neil Flow and were going up into the loft to sleep when they saw something looking in the window. They described it as a huge creature covered with hair from head to foot, and it left a large footprint in the snow as it ran away.

It should be noted that both men agreed the "creature" ran away, and had only looked in the window of the cabin.

Farrell and Springs went into either Blue Mountain Lake or Indian Lake and contacted Farrell's brother, Conservation Officer Jack Farrell. A posse was organized and went into the O'Neil Flow area to search for the "creature."

The group included seven persons and was under the command of Lt. Charles B. McCann of Troop B of the New York State Police. Also in the posse were: Trooper Addison Hall, Conservation Officer Jack Farrell, Ernest Blanchard and Charles Turner of Indian Lake and the two trappers, Farrell and Springs.

They returned to the cabin where the trappers had seen the wild man, and they followed tracks in the snow. The men said the tracks were about 30 inches long, very wide, and quite easy to follow in the deep snow.

On the second day of their search they came on a cabin in an old lumber camp near Dunbrook Mountain near the chain lakes in the Town of Newcomb. Known as Stanley Camp in Stanley Clearing, the area was quite open, and the men surrounded the camp.

Two of the men in the posse, in remembering the scene 44 years later said someone had called to the "creature" to come out of the camp and surrender, but it leaped through a window and tried to run away through the deep snow. They remembered it crouched by a log pile and reports from those present say there was an exchange of conversation.

The police officers called for the figure to surrender and to come out, but the wild man answered that he wanted to be left alone and told the group to go away.

As the posse advanced, the figure by the log pile fired a shotgun and Turner fell screaming in pain to the snow.

Two persons said they heard Lt. McCann yell an order to fire and a barrage of slugs cut the figure down.

While they agreed they had tried to aim for its arms and legs, they found they had killed the wild man. They found him dressed in numerous layers of untanned bear and deer skins, and when they stripped the huge man down, they found he was a five-foot- six-inch, 135-pound black man.

Turning their attention to the wounded Turner, they found that a slug from the wild man's shotgun had struck Turner in the hip. Turner had a silver dollar in his pocket, and the slug had struck the coin. Except for a nasty bruise, Turner was uninjured.

The men sent for Hamilton County Acting Coroner Dr. H.F. Carroll, who remembered walking more than 10 miles on snow shoes to reach the body.

"I was probably acting illegally," the then-retired doctor told us in 1976. Dr. Carroll was still living in Indian Lake when he remembered the trek into the woods to examine the body. "They chased him out of Hamilton County, and they had shot him in Essex County," Dr. Carroll said, "but he sure was dead."

Dr. Carroll's son John, who had become a Conservation Officer in Indian Lake, remembered that it was his toboggan that was brought into Stanley Clearing to bring out the body. The men waited until morning, and when they started to return to Indian Lake, the body had frozen stiff on the toboggan.

The body was brought to Burt Swain's Funeral Parlor in North Creek for an inquest, but as it thawed it had to be removed because of being wrapped in the several layers of untanned animal skins.

It was discovered the wild man had spent some time in the deep woods, killing deer and bear, and then sitting down and eating the raw meat on the hindquarters, just as an animal would after making a kill.

He reportedly had stolen rifle ammunition from lumber and hunting camps, and it was found he opened his shotgun shells, dumped out the birdshot and placed slugs from the rifle shell in the shotgun casings.

His shotgun must have been in one of the camps he was accused of burning down, since the stock had been burned away. He had rigged a wire to pull the trigger, using a wire he had taken from a hay bail he had found on a mountain farm.

The identity of the man was never discovered as he had no identification, and no one ever came forward to say they knew him. In addition to the burned shotgun, he was carrying $7 in Canadian money. There was a rumor at the time he was shot that he could have been a man missing from Syracuse, but that was never confirmed.

Hamilton County refused to put up the $75 to bury him, as county officials claimed he had been shot in Essex County. There are conflicting reports about the burial. Some persons say he was buried in Newcomb, but others insist he was taken to a Potters Field in a corner of a cemetery in North Creek and buried in an unmarked grave.

The large footprints were explained as police found he had wrapped his feet in many layers of bear skins making in effect, a snowshoe that allowed him to run over the surface of the snow and causing him to leave a large footprint, thus creating the term "Bigfoot" to describe his tracks.

Dr. Carroll said the men managed to pull the body the miles from Stanley Clearing to Indian Lake just in time. "We got a big snowstorm later that day and all the next," he remembered. "We must have got about two feet of snow over the two days."

Lt. McCann later retired from the State Police and lived with his daughter in Southeastern New York, living into his 90s. Trooper Addison Hall also retired and lived out his years in Western New York.

An examination of the body showed an old bullet wound to the head, and there was speculation that the old wound may have been the cause of the man going wild and moving into the interior of the Adirondacks to live off the land.

District Attorney McDonald reacted to a spate of local outrage about the shooting of the wild man with a long letter, which was made available by Attorney Robert W. Bascom of Hudson Falls.

Dated April 8, 1932, it states: "With reference to the shooting at Newcomb, it is a long story, but the facts are briefly as follows.

"Deceased was a very black negro, apparently between 25 and 30 years of age, five-feet-six inches in height and weighing approximately 135 pounds. He had been killed by a gunshot wound, which entered his abdomen near the sympathus pubis and emerged just over the right shoulder — wound at point of entry and exit small — apparently a rifle wound made by steel jacket bullet. There was a superficial wound just perforating the skin on the right leg midway between the knee and hip. Also a slight wound on the right side near the first floating rib. Cause of death, gunshot wound in the abdomen.

"About the first of March, two residents of Blue Mountain Lake Village were hunting foxes near or on the side of Blue Mountain when they came upon a strange track in the snow. Following it a short distance they saw a negro who was building a fire. On seeing them he ran toward them and when distant about 100 feet, pointed a gun at them and told them to get out. He said he didn't want to shoot them, but he would if they didn't go away. They then returned to Blue Mountain Lake and reported to the State Police. The following morning these two men, accompanied by a State Trooper named Hall and Merrit Lamos, Game Protector, went into the woods, took up the trail of the negro and followed it all day. At evening they were on Dunbar Mountain and had not come up with their quarry. They abandoned the track and went back home."

District Attorney McDonald continued in his long narrative: "The next day a party was organized consisting of Blanchard, Turner, Game Protectors Lamos and Farrell, Lt. McCann, Sergeant Skowyra and Troopers Hall and Donnellan. They went into O'Neil Flow Camp where they remained overnight, starting out before daylight the following morning and being joined by Richard Farrell, the caretaker at the camp. They again picked up the trail on Dunbar Mountain and followed it going in a general north-easterly direction, coming up with the negro between 11 and 12 o'clock at or near Donnelly Mountain in the Town of Newcomb. At this time, McCann and Donnellan had fallen back some mile or more from the party, and they were not present at the shooting.

"When the party came upon the negro, they called upon him to stop, stating they would not injure him, etc. However, the negro started to go away from them, and they attempted an encirclement of him, Turner succeeding in getting in front of him.

"At this time Turner and Lamos were both armed with 30-30 carbine rifles (loaded with steel jacket bullets) which the Troopers had been carrying, but which had been taken from them to aid them in traveling. The Troopers had their .45 service revolvers loaded with lead bullets, Protectors Lamos and Farrell had .38 revolvers and Richard Farrell had a shotgun. The negro was carrying a double-barrel shotgun and had a single-barrel shotgun slung over his shoulder.

"The posse started to close in on the negro, and he continued going in the direction of Turner. The negro then shot at Turner, who ducked behind a tree. He shot again, and then the party began shooting at him. One of the pellets from the negro's gun struck Turner on the hip and lodged in a pocket book. Turner states he does not know how many times he shot, but examination of his gun afterward revealed that he shot three times. The other members of the party, with the exception of Blanchard, fired several shots at the negro. Lamos did not shoot. The negro shot five times in all, and his attempted sixth shot at a Trooper, when they were quite close, failed to explode.

"The members of the posse stated that they shot at his arms and legs.

"After the first few shots, the negro dropped to his knees or squatted down, saying in effect, 'You got me that time boss, but I am going to fight until I die.' Apparently this must have been at the time he was wounded in the leg. He continued firing after this, and after a few more shots, fell over. The posse rushed up to him, and he was lying partly on his back. They tried to talk with him, but he did not answer, although they said he was still alive. Whether he was unable to speak, I do not know. The negro lived about four or five minutes.

"They then carried him down the Mountain to an old lumber camp. These camps were practically destroyed, one of the buildings had apparently burned a short time before. In this building was a box stove and the spring of a bed. There were a number of tracks about the building indicating that the negro had been staying there. In a root cellar they also found the recent remains of a small fire, the negro having stayed there after the main building burned. In was then past noon and as they were several miles from any road or camp they left the negro's body at the camp, putting him on a piece of roofing tin and covering him over with other tin. The snow was deep, and the country very rough.

"The following day, Blanchard and several other men went back with a toboggan and carried the body out.

"The negro was very poorly dressed. He wore three light sweaters on the upper part of his body and two pair of torn trousers on the lower part. The sweaters and trousers were much worn and torn, so much so that you could see his naked body through the clothes. The sweaters and trousers were burned and charred along the back indicating that he had probably fallen asleep too close to his fire.

"On his feet he had an old pair of rubber shoes, badly worn, around which had been wrapped deer skin with the hair side out and tied. Around his feet and inside the rubbers were two or three pieces of rags. His hands and arms to the elbows were bare. On his head he wore a knit cap of the type known as aviation cap which pulled over the head and face with an opening around the eyes.

"In his clothing they found an old harmonica, two shells, and seven one-dollar bills, also an old kitchen knife was fastened near his waist. Over his shoulder he carried a knapsack made from a burlap bag, which fastened by rope over his shoulders. In the knapsack were several cans, in one of which were some shotgun shells, one can contained grease or tallow, a third can contained about two-thirds of a pint of powder. Two cans contained matches.

"The shot had apparently been picked from the shells and some of them were loaded with what looked like rifle bullets which had been cut up into slugs.

"Richard Farrell, the caretaker at the O'Neil Flow Camp, stated that in the previous fall some shotgun shells disappeared from the Camp.

"Farrell further testified that a few nights before the negro was killed, he was awakened in the middle of the night by a noise and the reflection of a light in the window. Thinking that it was someone coming to the Camp he got up and hollered out, and whoever was there went away. The following morning he found two burned matches near the window and also tracks with deer hair in them which were similar to tracks the negro made in the snow.

"It is apparent that Turner fired the shot which killed the negro, as it would not seem that a revolver bullet, and particularly a lead one, could penetrate or leave as small an opening both at the point of entry and exit as the bullet which killed the negro.

"The foregoing is practically all the facts which developed. Lt. McCann testified that before starting out that morning that he had given instructions that the posse should be very careful in approaching the man if they came up to him, not to do any shooting until fired upon, and then only if necessary to protect themselves.

"We have done nothing further since the inquest, but from the facts developed, I do not see that criminal proceedings would avail anything."

This letter from the District Attorney was apparently meant to quiet a public outcry which developed in the area. There was outspoken opinion that the wild man had been hunted down, and since he had done nothing wrong, many asked why a posse of armed men had gone after him in the first place, when all he sought was to be left alone in the wilderness.

The height of the outcry had been an editorial in the Glens Falls daily newspaper, *The Post-Star*. Under a headline, "The Giant Is Dead," the morning newspaper stated: "In the due course of time an inquest will be held in Essex County in the case of the so-called 'giant wild man of the Adirondacks' who was recently the object of a State Police manhunt and was eventually brought out of the woods dead, the victim of a posse's gunfire.

"It seems to *The Post-Star* that this killing reflects discreditably upon the State Police.

"When this giant wild man of the Adirondacks was finally conquered it developed that he weighed 130 pounds and was five-feet-six inches tall. He wore several sweaters, which fact apparently was foundation for the belief that he was even more fearsome a person physically than the average State Policeman.

"The story of the incident given out by authorities to the press was, in brief, that the man was apparently a partially demented hermit or a refugee from justice. He had been seen attempting to break into cabins, and woodsmen said he had threatened harm to them on several occasions while they were engaged in visiting traps. So far as is generally known, he had committed no major crime. A posse went after him, found him in the woods north of Newcomb, and ordered him to surrender. He is reported to have fired one shot, which rent the clothing of one of the Troopers. The posse returned fire, aiming at his legs, but the man dropped down behind a clump of bushes and one of the shots, instead of entering a leg, found his body and killed him.

"We think the killing was unnecessary and unwarranted. It seems to us that half a dozen officers, supposedly trained in effecting captures of unruly persons, should have been able to overpower this individual without harming him or at the very worst to have subdued him with minor wounds. The feeling that many people have is that the officials unnecessarily killed an unfortunate person whose station in life, they were aware, was not such as would result in influential survivors protesting the act violently after he was dead.

"It is possible, even likely, that this man had committed no worse crime than being mentally ill. Are we then to assume that any person who may become ill, mentally or otherwise, and do eccentric things, must be in danger of State Police bullets?

"Must we think of our State Police as men who are not willing to take the personal risks which are supposed to be a part of their duty, who in an emergency will shoot first and think it over after they have laid their man low?

"Are we to respect our State Police, or are they to arouse in our minds the emotions of disgust and fear?

"For the sake of an efficient policing of the state, and in the name of a reasonably humane social attitude toward breakers of the law, we protest the slaying of the giant of the Adirondacks and demand that such methods no longer characterize the service of the guardians of society."

There are consistencies and many inconsistencies in the stories of how the giant of the Adirondacks died. The District Attorney's letter seems in keeping with the "official" story of the day, while the memories of the men involved told years afterward show a different story.

The complete details will never be known. Much of the story died with the 130-pound, five-foot-six inch wild man and lies in an unmarked grave in either Newcomb or North Creek.

Editor's Note: The following poem was published following the shooting of a person described as the Adirondack Wild Man or Giant of the Adirondacks sometime in late February 1932. The author of the poem signed it only J.O.S. and is unknown.

"Giant" negro slain by State Troopers at Newcomb proved to be five-feet-six inches tall and to weigh one hundred and thirty pounds.

- News Item.

John Brown, sleeping on Elba Hill
Is it true that your spirit is marching still?

_____

Through the County of Essex the word has spread
That a giant negro, who towered a head
Above the height of the average man
Was roaming the mountains; of course he ran
When he saw a stranger, but no one knew
Just where he came from or what he'd do.
He lived alone, in a lumber camp,
He might be a killer or just a tramp.
So they thought it well he be hunted down
Ere he came in body to raid a town.

Old Essex men were a hardy breed
Who never had felt an urgent need
Of running a stranger into the earth.
They ran their own lives and knew the worth
Of solitude. If a man was right
He might be colored -he might be white-
They left him alone to his own affairs
So he didn't interfere with theirs.

But the negro lived in a camp in the wood
And shot and fished for his daily food.
It's not long since we all did the same
When the forests were teeming with fish and game
When there were no licenses, guards or guides
And the first growth covered the mountain sides.

Well, the negro "giant" worried along
But he kept to himself -which no doubt was wrong,
For they sought him out, a party of ten,
Guides, Troopers, Police -all hardy men.
They tracked him down to his shack in the wood
And shouted "Surrender" though why he should
It doesn't appear in the published tale,
And why he should go to the local jail
Is a mystery yet to be made quite clear;
So they shot him down as they'd shoot a deer.
But when they went to measure the game
They found he didn't bulk quite the same
He had shrunk so much from his rumored size
That they "shot at his knees" but they hit his eyes.
He was five feet six in his sandals dirty
And his weight was about one hundred thirty.
It's the biggest game that gets away,
But the hunters called it a Perfect Day.

Wake, John Brown!
For freedom has gone from the mountain and plain
And it's time that your spirit should walk again!

J.O.S.

INDEX